&

You

Invincible Publication Pvt Ltd.

Published by:

Invincible Publication Pvt Ltd.
201A, SAS Tower, Sector 38, Gurugram, Haryana – 122003
Phone: +91-124-4034247, +91 9599066061
Website : www.invinciblepublishers.com

Sales Office : - 4760-61/23, Basement, Pratap Street, Ansari Road, Daryaganj, New Delhi - 110002
Phone: +91-11-40198405
Email: invinciblepublishers@gmail.com

This book is a work of academic. Names, characters, places and incidents are either the product of the author's imagination or are used fictitiously. Any resemblance to real persons, living or dead, or actual events or locations, is purely coincidental and the publisher does not hold responsibility for the same.

ISBN : 978-81-963918-6-7

Book Name : Money and You

First Edition: May 2023

Introduction

Building a Strong Relationship with Money

by

Dr. Mukul Agrawal

Money & You

Have you ever wondered how your life is impacted by money?

Are you hoping to establish a happy and successful relationship with your money? Look nowhere else! In "Money & You," I have tried to offer a thorough manual to aid young people in comprehending and navigating the realm of personal finance.

I will lead you on a journey towards financial empowerment by drawing on my own 2- decades of experience and knowledge. This book aims to demystify difficult financial ideas and make them understandable to people from all walks of life. This book will give you the information and skills you need to make wise financial decisions, whether you're a student, a recent graduate, or just starting out in your financial life.

From setting up a budget and saving money to investing and accumulating wealth, "Money & You" covers a wide range of topics. I have made an effort to offer real-world examples and doable solutions to assist you in managing your money well.

This book will teach you how to make a budget, set financial goals, and form sound spending practices. As I show you how to make your money work for you, I also go into the realm of investments. You will learn tips for handling debt and making plans for a stable financial future.

The focus of "Money & You" is cultivating a good attitude towards money rather than merely talking about computations and numbers. I attempted to inspire readers to develop a positive connection with money by emphasizing both their financial security and leading fulfilling lives.

"Money & You" is the best resource to help you on your path to financial independence, whether your goal is to conquer financial obstacles, accumulate riches, or simply take control over your finances.

Let me be your dependable travel companion while I impart my knowledge and give you the tools you need to manage your money.

Be Prepared to have your relationship with money transformed by "Money & You".

FINANCIAL
LITERACY
TAX

Contents

About Author

Dr. Mukul Agrawal: Improving Lives Through Finance

Dear Reader

I am Dr. Mukul Agrawal, a seasoned financial expert with 19 years of business expertise. I feel honored to have been named the "Largest Financial Investment Lesson" Guinness World Record holder and fortunate to have talked at esteemed venues like TEDx and JoshTalk.

My journey has been devoted to helping people through financial education. My goal is to make personal finance understandable to everyone as a best-selling author, trainer, and investor. I have helped over 2 million people achieve financial freedom through my books, training courses, and a vibrant online community.

I am incredibly proud to have mentored over 40,000 students and seen their dreams come true. My aim is to offer individuals practical strategies to reach their financial objectives by demystifying complicated financial topics.

Everyone should have the resources and knowledge necessary to make wise financial decisions since it is a fundamental right. Come along with me as we navigate the complexity of personal finance, face obstacles, and seize opportunities on this transformative path to financial well- being.

I'm here to help, advise, and inspire you to take charge of your financial future. Let's set out on a path to development, success, and financial wealth together.

With sincere regards,

Dr. Mukul Agrawal

Dr. Mukul Agrawal

CHAPTER

One

Understanding the value of money and the basics of personal finance

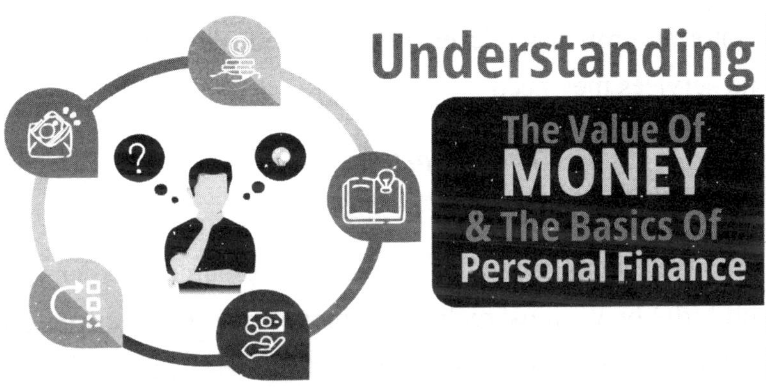

What is Money?

Money is a legal tender that acts as a resource that we utilize to purchase goods we require or desire. Coins, paper bills, or digital currency are all examples of legal tender. Due to the widespread acceptance that money has worth, trading between individuals is made simpler.

Here are a few instances of money in Indian culture:

Coins

Coins are the oldest form of currency in India. They have long been employed as a medium of commerce.

In the 18th century, **paper money** first appeared in India. It is currently the currency that is most commonly used in India.

Digital currency: Using digital currency is a relatively new concept. Even though it is still not widely accepted in India, it is becoming more and more popular.

Much of the economy depends on money. It promotes economic growth while enabling individuals to buy the goods and services they need.

The Importance of Money

We require money as a necessary resource in order to live comfortably. We must realize that money does not just appear out of thin air; rather, we must work hard and wisely to obtain it. We need money to buy food, clothing, and housing, so it's crucial to set aside some cash for unforeseen costs.

For example, we won't be able to eat and may go without food if we don't have enough cash to buy food. We might not be able to stay warm in cold weather if we don't have enough money to buy clothes.

Let's think about a specific illustration:

Consider a family that resides in a village. Their main source of revenue comes from agriculture. To raise crops and make money, they put a lot of effort into their farms. However, unanticipated events like a drought or crop failure have a significant impact on their annual income.

As a result, they are in a predicament where they are unable to provide their family with food. They struggle to meet their basic dietary demands and are unable to afford necessary food. Their inability to eat and keep good health is strongly impacted by their financial situation.

Additionally, the family is unable to set aside money to buy warm clothing. They are unprepared for the brisk winter weather that has arrived with the arrival of autumn. Discomfort, health problems, and potential illnesses result from this.

In this case, the family's capacity to meet their fundamental necessities is directly impacted by the lack of money. It emphasizes how important financial stability is in ensuring access to necessities like clothing and food, which are crucial for both survival and wellbeing.

Managing Money

Once you understand the Importance of Money. You need to manage your hard earned money.

Making the most of our resources is the definition of managing money. We must learn how to budget, which entails determining how much cash we can set up for the future and how much we must spend on necessities. We should also refrain from splurging on things we don't actually need and instead concentrate on making investments to increase our wealth.

If we receive Rs. 10 per week as an allowance or from a part-time job, for instance, we should budget how much we want to spend on entertainment, food, and other costs.

In order to comprehend the idea of managing money, let's look at a straightforward example:

Meet Rahul, a young professional living and working in a large Indian metropolis. He has a respectable income and wants to guarantee that he gets the most out of it.

Rahul begins with making a budget in order to efficiently manage his finances. He meticulously figures out how much money he makes each month and makes a list of all his necessary expenditures, including rent, utilities, groceries, transportation, and loan payments. Depending on the significance of each category, he gives it a certain amount of money.

Rahul resolves to save a percentage of his income for the future after putting money aside for necessities. He creates a savings account and decides to set aside a particular amount of his monthly income for savings. In the long run, this will assist him in reaching his financial objectives and serve as an emergency fund.

Rahul lists his discretionary expenditures in order to prevent irrational spending. He understands that he frequently spends a sizable sum of money on dining out and entertainment.

Even though he enjoys these hobbies, he decides to cut down and devote less of his budget to these luxuries. This enables him to increase his savings and improve his financial management.

Rahul investigates investing opportunities since he recognises the value of seeing his money increase. He starts putting some of his savings in mutual funds after learning about them. He hopes to achieve returns on his assets and gradually accumulate riches by doing this.

Rahul discovers that he has a better grasp on his finances as he keeps using prudent money management. He is able to save money for the future, pay his bills in a comfortable manner, and even increase his fortune through investments. Rahul now has financial security and mental tranquility as a result of his smart money management.

This illustration highlights the value of setting a budget, conserving money, staying out of debt, and making smart investments.

Types of Accounts

We can manage our finances using a variety of account kinds. Our money is safe and earns interest in a savings account. A checking account is helpful for handling regular expenses like paying bills or for shopping. In an emergency, credit cards can be useful, but they should be used wisely to prevent debt.

For instance, you could utilize a savings account to put money aside for future costs like a car or vacation. A checking account can be used for regular expenditures like paying bills or for grocery shopping.

To better comprehend the idea of managing money using various sorts of accounts, let's look at a straightforward example:

Meet Priya, a working woman who aspires to handle her money wisely. She makes the decision to manage her money effectively by using several sorts of accounts.

Priya begins by opening a savings account with a bank. She consistently transfers a portion of her money into this account. Her savings account contains money that is secure and accrues interest over time. Priya intends to utilize this account to put money down for future costs like a car or vacation. She guarantees that she will have money on hand when she needs it by setting money aside in her savings account, where it also accrues interest.

In addition, Priya opens a checking account. She can conduct her daily financial operations with this account easily. She manages her usual costs, pays her bills, and purchases groceries using her checking account. Priya can keep track of her expenditures and retain a clear image of her available cash by using a separate account for these transactions. She has convenient access to her money through the checking account, enabling her to carry out transactions.

Priya also takes into account using credit cards in addition to her savings and checking accounts. She is aware that credit cards might be useful for making significant expenditures or in dire circumstances. She utilizes her credit cards properly and with caution. Priya makes sure she fully settles her credit card bill each month to prevent accruing unneeded debt. She can take advantage of the ease and security that credit cards offer by using them responsibly while avoiding getting into financial trouble.

Priya uses this example to show how various account types may be used to successfully manage money. She manages her finances by keeping regular costs in a checking account, saving for long-term goals in a savings account, and using credit cards sparingly for big purchases or unexpected expenses. Priya uses this strategy to keep her money under control, save savings, and stay away from taking on too much debt.

This illustration emphasizes the significance of selecting the appropriate accounts for various financial needs, utilizing them sensibly, and preserving financial stability.

Investments

When we invest, we want to see a long-term increase in the value of our money. Common investment alternatives include stocks, bonds, and mutual funds. Before putting our money into these alternatives, it's critical to do some study and comprehend the hazards.

If we invest Rs. 100 in a stock, for instance, and the business succeeds, the stock's value could rise to Rs. 120. The shares can then be sold for a profit of Rs. 20. The stock value could fall and we could lose money, though, if the business performs poorly.

To better comprehend the idea of investments and their

prospective returns, let's look at a straightforward example:

Consider Ravi, a new investor in India, who chooses to put 100 rupees into the stock market. He is aware of the hazards and has researched numerous investing options.

Ravi decides to buy stock in a specific business. The value of the stock could rise over time if the business does well. Suppose the stock's price increases to Rs. 120. Now that he has made this decision, Ravi decides to sell the shares, making a profit of Rs. 20. The return on his investment is this profit.

However, there is always a chance that the business won't operate as anticipated. The stock's value can drop if the company does poorly. Assume that the stock drops to Rs. 80. In this case, Ravi would lose Rs. 20 if he decided to sell the shares.

This illustration shows the gains and hazards of stock investing. Stock prices can change depending on a number of variables, including business performance, market conditions, and investor sentiment. While profitable investments can result in gains, there is also the chance that losses could be incurred if the assets do not perform well.

It's important to keep in mind that investing entails some degree of risk, therefore it's essential to do extensive study and fully comprehend the dangers before making investment selections. Investors can reduce risks and perhaps raise the likelihood of long-term profitable returns by diversifying their holdings among a variety of asset types, such as stocks, bonds, and mutual funds.

In addition to emphasizing the value of thorough analysis, risk assessment, and taking into account potential returns and losses connected with investments, this example offers a simpler understanding of investing in stocks.

Setting Goals

We can maintain our motivation and concentrate on money management by setting financial goals. We can establish both short-term and long-term objectives, such as saving for a new phone or retirement. We may track our progress and experience a sense of accomplishment when we reach our goals by setting them.

For instance, we can decide to buy a new video game and save Rs. 50 as our short-term objective. When we attain our target, we may then measure our success by setting aside Rs. 5 each week for 10 weeks. We might also establish a long-term objective of saving Rs. 1,000 for college expenses and work towards that objective by setting aside a portion of our weekly wages or allowance.

To better grasp the idea of having financial goals and managing money, let's look at a specific example:

Neha is a teen who strives to cultivate wise financial practices. Neha is aware of the value of setting financial objectives in order to maintain her drive and commitment to her journey towards sound money management.

Neha first decides to spend Rs. 500 on a brand-new video game as a short-term objective. In order to achieve her aim, she resolves to set aside Rs. 50 from her weekly stipend. Neha keeps track of her development by budgeting Rs. 5 for ten weeks. She sees her funds increase as she consistently saves, which inspires her to keep practicing wise money management. Neha enjoys buying the video game when she finally accomplished her goal of Rs. 500 and feels successful.

Neha also establishes a long-term objective of saving Rs. 1,000 for her future college expenditures in order to improve her money management abilities. She makes the decision to designate a portion of her weekly salary or stipend for this purpose. Neha dutifully sets aside a set sum each week and monitors her growth over time. She develops better money management skills and a greater appreciation for the value of setting aside money for future needs as she persistently works towards her long-term objective.

Setting both short-term and long-term financial objectives helps Neha form the habit of prioritizing and planning her spending. She gains an appreciation for delayed pleasure and experiences the joy of reaching her financial goals. Neha finds that having financial objectives keeps her focused, motivated, and enables her to make wise financial decisions.

This illustration shows the need of having financial goals for various time periods, whether they are near-term aims like purchasing a video game or far-reaching targets like saving for college costs. It emphasizes how crucial it is to monitor your progress, acknowledge your successes, and use goal-setting as a tool for efficient money management.

Benefits of Personal Finance

Numerous advantages can result from understanding personal finance. We can experience a greater sense of financial control and less anxiety due to unforeseen expenses. Additionally, there may be more chances for us to accomplish our objectives, such as house ownership or international vacation. We can have better and more satisfying lives if we manage our money well.

For instance, good money management can help us avoid debt and provide us greater financial freedom to follow our goals, such as traveling or starting a business. Additionally, we can have additional protection in the event that we incur unforeseen costs, such as auto or medical expenditures.

To further comprehend the idea of personal finance and its advantages, let's look at a specific example:

Meet Rina, a recent graduate who makes the decision to manage her personal finances. Rina can benefit from a variety of advantages by understanding personal finance, many of which will improve her quality of life.

In the beginning, Rina learns sound money management techniques that assist her in avoiding unneeded debt. She makes a budget to keep track of her earnings and outgoing costs and make sure she lives within her means. Rina doesn't rack up credit card debt or take out loans she can't afford to pay back because she sticks to her budget. She feels at ease and in charge of her money because of her financial discipline.

Rina benefits from more financial freedom to follow her goals and objectives as a result of good money management. She envisions, for instance, one day opening her own business and visiting several nations. Rina is able to set aside money from her income for these objectives by practicing sound money management. She looks into inexpensive trip choices, establishes a travel budget, and starts saving accordingly. Similar to this, Rina develops a savings strategy to amass the funds required to launch her own company. She can confidently pursue these goals without being constrained by money by managing her money well.

Furthermore, Rina has a safety net for unplanned spending because of her knowledge of personal finance. She is aware of the value of setting up an emergency fund to pay for unforeseen expenses like auto repairs or medical expenses. Every month, Rina transfers a portion of her income into a special savings account for unplanned expenses. She feels secure and can deal with unforeseen circumstances with less worry and financial strain because of this financial cushion.

In this illustration, Rina sees the advantages of knowing personal finance. She takes charge of her finances, stays out of debt, and has the flexibility to go after her desires and goals. Additionally, Rina feels secure knowing that she is ready for unanticipated costs.

Rina enjoys a more contented and meaningful life as a result of good money management. She can live in the moment while putting effort into securing her financial future. This illustration demonstrates how wise money management can result in increased financial security, decreased stress, and the capacity to confidently pursue a happy life.

CHAPTER Two

Setting financial goals and creating a budget

Developing a budget and setting financial objectives are crucial components of managing personal finances. In the Indian context, the following procedures can be taken to identify financial objectives and construct a budget:

1. **Assess your current financial situation:** Consider your income, expenses, debts, and assets as you examine your present financial condition. List every source of income you have, including your salary, company income, rental income, and any additional sources. List all of your

expenses as well, including both fixed and variable costs like rent, utilities, insurance, and groceries, entertainment, and travel.

2. **Set financial goals:** Establish financial goals that are SMART—specific, measurable, realistic, relevant, and time-bound—based on your current financial condition. For instance, you could wish to put money aside for your retirement, your child's education, or a down payment on a house.

3. **Prioritize your goals:** After you've determined your financial goals, rank them in order of significance. For instance, saving for your child's education can be your top priority if they will be entering college in five years. Saving for retirement should also be a top priority if you intend to retire within the next ten years.

4. **Create a budget:** List all of your income and cost sources to develop a budget. Include every expense, even the smallest ones like coffee or snacks. Spend a portion of your income on your spending and financial objectives. For instance, set aside a certain sum each month for your child's education if you wish to save for it.

5. **Track your spending:** Track your expenditures after you've made a budget to make sure you're staying within it. To keep track of your spending, try a budgeting tool like MoneyControl, Walnut, or Monefy. Regularly review your budget, and then make any required adjustments.

Here's an example of how this could work:

Assume you have the following monthly costs and a monthly income of 50,000:

Rent:	Rs. 10,000
Utilities:	Rs. 5,000
Groceries:	Rs. 8,000
Entertainment:	Rs. 3,000
Transportation:	Rs. 4,000
Credit card payment:	Rs. 2,000

Your financial goals are:

Save Rs. 2 lakh for a down payment on a home in two years

Save Rs. 3 lakh for your child's education in five years

Save Rs. 5 lakh for retirement in 10 years

To achieve these goals, you could create a budget as follows:

Allocate Rs. 10,000 per month towards your down payment goal.

Allocate Rs. 5,000 per month towards your child's education goal.

Allocate Rs. 5,000 per month towards your retirement goal.

Allocate the remaining income towards your expenses, which would be Rs. 30,000 per month.

You may accomplish your financial objectives while still properly managing your costs if you stick to this budget.

CHAPTER

Three

Tracking income and expenses

Keeping track of income and expenses is crucial to managing personal finances. In order to track income and expenses in the Indian setting, the following procedures can be taken:

Keeping track of all sources of revenue: Start by keeping track of all of your sources of income. Included in this are a person's salary, business profits, rental income, interest income, and any other kinds of income. Make sure to note the sum and date of each source of income.

Track all expenses: Keep track of every penny you spend, including both fixed costs like rent, electricity, and insurance and variable costs like groceries, entertainment, and travel. Make sure to note each expense's amount and date.

Categorize expenses: Sort your spending according to various categories, such as lodging, travel, meals, entertainment, and so forth. You can use this to analyze your spending habits and find areas where you can reduce your spending.

Use a budgeting app: To keep track of your income and expenses, use a budgeting tool or piece of software. In India, there are many budgeting applications accessible, including Paytm and Moneymanger. You may enter and categorize your income and expenses using these apps. They also assist you stick to your budget by giving you useful insights on your spending habits.

Review your spending regularly: To make sure that you are staying inside your budget, periodically review your spending. Find out where your expenditure may be excessive and search for solutions to reduce it. For instance, you can try cooking more frequently at home if you find that you are spending too much money eating out.

Here is an illustration of how this might function:

Assume you have the following monthly costs and a monthly income of Rs. 50,000

Rent:	Rs. 10,000
Utilities:	Rs. 5,000
Groceries:	Rs. 8,000

Entertainment: Rs. 3,000

Transportation: Rs. 4,000

Credit card payment: Rs. 2,000

You might use a budgeting programme like Money Manager to keep tabs on your earnings and outgoing costs.

You would enter your sources of income and expenses into the programme and group them into the following categories:

Housing: Rs. 10,000 (rent)

Utilities: Rs. 5,000 (electricity, water, gas, etc.)

Food: Rs. 8,000 (groceries, dining out)

Entertainment: Rs. 3,000 (movies, shopping, etc.)

Transportation: Rs. 4,000 (fuel, public transportation, etc.)

Debt: Rs. 2,000 (credit card payment)

Your spending patterns would then be usefully revealed by the app, including how much you are spending on each category and how your spending stacks up against your budget. With the help of this knowledge, you can make wise financial decisions and adhere to your spending plan.

CHAPTER Four

Saving and investing money

Investing and saving money are crucial components of financial planning. The following actions can be taken to invest and save money:

1. **Set financial goals:** Setting financial objectives is the first step in saving and investing money. These objectives may be short-term, like saving for a trip or a down payment on a home, or long-term, like saving for retirement or the

education of your children.

2. **Create a budget:** A budget is necessary for conserving money. Every month, you should set aside some of your money for savings and investing. It's a good idea to set aside at least 10% of your salary for savings.

2. **Choose the right savings account:** A savings account with a high interest rate is the best option. Regular savings accounts, fixed deposits, and recurring deposits are just a few of the various types of savings accounts that are offered in India.

2. **Invest in mutual funds:** In India, mutual funds are a well-liked form of investment. With a very little sum of money, they enable you to invest in a diverse portfolio of equities and bonds. Mutual funds come in a variety of forms, including balanced, debt, and equity funds.

2. **Invest in stocks:** Long-term profits on stock investments can be very substantial. It can be risky though, so it's crucial to conduct your research and choose stocks with a proven track record.

2. **Invest in real estate:** Another well-liked investment choice in India is real estate. By purchasing a home or contributing to a real estate fund, you can invest in real estate.

Here's an example of how this could work:

Again assume that you have a monthly income of Rs. 50,000 and you want to save and invest 10% of your income each month.

Here's how you could allocate your savings:

Savings account:	Rs. 5,000 (10% of income)
Mutual funds:	Rs. 3,000 (6% of income)
Stocks: Rs.	2,000 (4% of income)

A fixed deposit account, for example, is a savings option with a high interest rate. You might put money into a balanced mutual fund with a successful track record.

For stocks, you may buy blue-chip stocks with a track record of generating solid returns.

You can gradually increase the amount you save and invest each month as your income rises. To make sure you are on pace to reach your financial objectives, it's also crucial to routinely analyze your investments and make adjustments as necessary.

CHAPTER
Five

Making wise spending decisions

Making wise financial decisions is essential to preserving financial stability. The following actions can be taken to make wise financial decisions:

1. **Set a budget:** Making wise financial decisions begins with creating a budget. This entails keeping track of your spending and dividing it up into other categories, such as entertainment, food, and travel.

2. **Prioritize needs over wants:** It's critical to distinguish between needs and wants. Food, shelter, and clothing are

examples of necessities, whereas desires are products that are desirable but not necessities. Making wise financial decisions will involve giving needs priority over wants.

2. **Comparison shopping:** It's critical to compare costs and product or service quality before making a purchase. Finding the best value for your money can be aided by this.

2. **Don't make impulsive purchases:** Purchases made on a whim can result in overspending and financial strain. Before making a purchase, it is crucial to consider whether it is necessary and whether it will help you achieve your financial objectives.

2. **Use discounts and coupons:** Coupons and discounts can enable shoppers to save money. Utilize coupons when available and keep an eye out for promotions and discounts.

Here's an example of how this could work:

Assume that you have a monthly budget of Rs. 20,000 for your household expenses. Here's how you could allocate your budget:

Groceries: Rs. 7,000 (35% of budget)

Transportation: Rs. 3,000 (15% of budget)

Rent: Rs. 5,000 (25% of budget)

Entertainment: Rs. 2,000 (10% of budget)

Miscellaneous expenses: Rs. 3,000 (15% of budget)

Your needs should take precedence over your wants if you want to spend money wisely. To save money on groceries, you can decide to cook at home rather than go out to eat. To save money on transportation, you might also opt to use public transportation rather than purchase a car.

You could evaluate the costs and the quality of a product or service before making a purchase. To save money, you might also hunt for deals and coupons. You can make wise financial decisions, stick to your spending limit, and still lead a fulfilling life by doing so.

CHAPTER Six

Differentiating between needs and wants

When it comes to budgeting in India, it's critical to distinguish between needs and wants.

Here is an illustration of how to distinguish between wants and needs:

Things that are necessary for survival or daily existence are referred to as needs.

For instance: Basic needs including clothing, food, and

shelter.

Medical costs, such as prescription drugs, doctor visits, and health insurance.

Costs associated with education, such as textbooks, stationary, and tuition.

Utilities of bare need like gas, electricity, and water.

Expenses related to traveling to work or education by transport.

Wants are things that are desired but not necessary.

For instance: Expensive devices and gadgets.

Accessories and garments of high fashion.

Eating at upscale eateries.

Taking regular trips to far-off places.

Buying pricey goods or luxury vehicles.

Here's an example of how to prioritize needs over wants:

Assume that you have a monthly income of Rs. 50,000.

Prioritize meeting your necessities first, then spend the remainder on your wants.

For example, you could allocate your expenses as follows:

Basic necessities: Rs. 15,000 (30% of income)

Health-related expenses: Rs. 5,000 (10% of income)

Education-related expenses: Rs. 5,000 (10% of income)

Basic utilities: Rs. 5,000 (10% of income)

Transportation expenses: Rs. 5,000 (10% of income)

Savings and investments: Rs. 10,000 (20% of income)

Wants: Rs. 5,000 (10% of income)

You may make sure that you are covering your necessary expenses and setting aside money for the future by placing needs before wants.

You can still indulge in some of your wants, but it's crucial to stay within your budget.

This can assist you in achieving financial stability and help you stay away from pointless debt or financial stress.

CHAPTER
Seven

Understanding credit and debt

Credit and debt are crucial to the economy because they provide people and businesses access to money that they otherwise may not have.

To use credit and debt responsibly and prevent financial difficulties, it is crucial to comprehend how they function in the Indian environment.

The capacity to access money on credit from financial institutions including banks, non-banking financial corporations (NBFCs), and credit card issuers is referred to as having credit.

Credit is typically granted based on the creditworthiness of a person or firm, which is established by variables like their credit history, income, and assets.

Debt is the sum of money that a person or organization owes to a lender or creditor, usually plus interest. Credit card debt, personal loans, mortgages, and business loans are just a few of the many ways that people accumulate debt.

Credit and debt products come in a variety of forms, including:

Personal Loans: Personal loans are unsecured loans that can be used for many things, such as paying for a wedding, house improvements, or medical costs. The amount that can be borrowed depends on the borrower's income and creditworthiness, and these loans often have fixed interest rates and repayment terms.

Example: Let's say Anu wants to renovate her house, but she doesn't have the funds to pay for it. She may submit an application for a personal loan with a bank or NBFC. If she complies with the lender's eligibility requirements and has good credit, she might be granted a loan of, say, Rs. 5 lakhs at a fixed interest rate of 12% annually. She will then be required to pay back the loan in monthly installments over a 3 year, including both principal and interest.

Home Loans: Home loans are secured loans used to build or purchase homes. When compared to other loan kinds, these loans normally have lower interest rates, and the repayment duration might last up to 30 years.

Example: Say Ravi wants to spend Rs. 50 lakhs on a house. He may submit an application for a mortgage with a bank or housing finance firm. His application for a loan of, say, Rs. 40 lakhs at an interest rate of 8% annually may be allowed if he satisfies the lender's eligibility requirements and has a high credit score. He will have to pay back the loan in monthly installments for a total of 20 years, which will cover both the principal and interest.

Business Loans: Business loans are financial aid given to start a new company or grow an existing one. Depending on the lender and the borrower's creditworthiness, these loans can be secured or unsecured, and the interest rates and payback conditions change.

Example: Let's say Ram is an entrepreneur who wants to grow his modest company. An NBFC or bank may accept his application for a business loan. He might be given approval for a loan of, say, Rs. 10 lakhs at an interest rate of 15% per year if his company has a solid track record and he satisfies the lender's eligibility requirements. He must pay back the loan over a five-year term in equal monthly installments that cover both the principal and interest. Among other things, the loan might be used to buy new machinery, recruit more people, or enter new markets.

Credit Cards: People can borrow money on credit with credit cards up to a pre-set limit, making them a sort of revolving credit. When a balance on a credit card is not paid in full each month, the interest costs can pile up quickly. Credit cards frequently have high interest rates.

Example: If Priya doesn't have enough cash on hand, she wants to buy a new smartphone for Rs. 20,000. She is able to pay for the item with her credit card. She can make the purchase and pay off the sum over time if she has a credit limit of Rs. 30,000 and a credit card with an annual interest rate of 24%. She will be charged interest if she doesn't pay the entire balance by the due date, which can quickly mount up and put her in debt.

Gold Loans: Gold loans are secured loans that are provided in exchange for gold as security. Due to the prevalence of households with gold assets that can be used as collateral for loans, these loans are well-liked in India.

Example: Let's say Rohit needs money to cover his child's tuition but doesn't want to take out a high-interest personal loan. He can apply to a bank or NBFC for a gold loan. He can use gold jewelry worth Rs. 1 lakh as security to obtain a loan of, say, Rs. 70,000 at a 12% annual interest rate. He will be required to pay back the loan in monthly installments over the course of six months, which will include both principal and interest. His gold jewelry will be taken by the lender to recoup the unpaid balance if he is unable to make the loan payment on time.

It is crucial to manage debt and credit properly because defaulting on loans can result in fines, taxes, and harm to one's credit report.

Only borrow what is necessary, and have a set repayment strategy in place before taking out a loan, to prevent getting into debt. Before choosing a loan, it’s crucial to shop around and evaluate the interest rates and costs charged by various lenders.

CHAPTER Eight

Developing responsible financial habits

For long-term financial stability and security, it is essential to develop good financial practices. Here are some illustrations of sound financial practices to develop:

Creating a Budget: As I already explained multiple times, creating a budget is crucial. The cornerstone of responsible money management is budgeting. It entails keeping track of all your earnings and outgoing costs to ensure that you don't spend more than you make. It's crucial to develop a budget that takes into account your income, expenses, and financial objectives.

Example: Rajesh receives a monthly income of Rs. 60,000. He makes a budget and divides up his income into three categories: essentials like rent, food, and bills; discretionary, like entertainment and eating out; and savings and investments.

Saving Money: To attain long-term financial goals and create a financial safety net for emergencies, it is crucial to acquire the habit of saving money. You can begin by allocating a portion of your monthly income to savings, and then over time, progressively increase your savings rate.

For Example, Priya decides to save Rs. 1 lakh over the following six months. She begins by saving 5,000 rupees from her 50,000 rupee monthly income and progressively raises it to 10,000 rupees every month.

Investing Wisely: Another crucial financial habit is making prudent financial investments. Starting with low-risk investments like fixed deposits or recurring deposits, you can then progressively transition to higher-risk investments like mutual funds or equities. It's crucial to conduct your homework and pick investments that match your financial objectives and risk appetite.

Rohit, **for example**, wants to invest in mutual funds but has never done so before. He begins by looking into the past performance of several kinds of mutual funds. He decides on a diversified equities mutual fund with a strong track record and contributes Rs. 5,000 every month via a SIP.

Avoiding Debt: A crucial financial habit is avoiding

pointless debt. While getting a loan or using a credit card may be advantageous in some circumstances, it's crucial to refrain from using credit to fund frivolous purchases or a lifestyle beyond your means. If you decide to take on debt, be sure to have a strategy in place to pay it off as quickly as you can.

Nisha wants to purchase a new smartphone but doesn't have the cash on hand to do so. She decides against financing the purchase with her credit card and instead decides to save enough for it over a few months.

Monitoring Your Credit Score: Your credit score plays a significant role in determining how creditworthy and financially responsible you are. It's crucial to frequently check your credit score and, if necessary, take action to raise it. Some of these actions include paying off outstanding debt and completing all required payments on schedule. In the future, you may be able to get better credit card and loan conditions thanks to this, saving you money on interest and fees.

Example: Arjun regularly checks his credit score and discovers that it is lower than he anticipated. When he checks his credit report, he discovers an unpaid bill that he had previously overlooked. He quickly settles it and ensures that moving ahead, all of his payments will be made on schedule.

Planning for Retirement: Retirement planning is yet another crucial financial habit. You may get started by deciding what you want out of retirement and calculating how much money you'll need to get there. A retirement plan like a Provident Fund (PF), National Pension System (NPS), or Employee Provident

Fund (EPF) is a good place to start accumulating money for your golden years.

For Example, Deepak, who is 35 years old, wishes to retire with a retirement fund of Rs. 2 crore by the time he reaches 60. He calculates that in order to reach this goal, he will need to save Rs. 25,000 every month for the next 25 years. To reach his retirement objectives, he begins investing in a retirement plan like the National Pension System (NPS).

You can long-term acquire financial stability, security, and freedom by developing these sound financial practices.

CHAPTER Nine

Reflecting on financial decisions and learning from mistakes

For financial success and stability, it is essential to think back on financial choices and learn from failures. To ensure that you can reach your financial goals, it is crucial to comprehend the significance of prudent money management and making judgments.

In India, one of the biggest mistakes people make is failing to save enough money for the future. Many people have a tendency to spend all of their money without taking future demands like retirement, crises, or unforeseen bills into account. When these needs materialize later in life, this may cause financial challenges.

Making poor investment decisions is another prevalent error. Many people make high-risk investments without being aware of the potential risks. This could have a negative effect on their long-term financial stability and result in considerable losses.

Individuals who reflect on their financial choices might recognise their errors and apply what they've learned. It is crucial to assess the decision-making procedure and comprehend the variables that affected the choices. This can assist people in making wiser selections and preventing them from repeating their errors in the future.

Making wise financial decisions can be aided by both reflection and seeking financial counsel. Individuals can learn more about financial planning and investment possibilities by speaking with a wealth manager or financial advisor. This can help them reach their financial objectives.

It takes commitment and determination to continuously learn from financial blunders. To maintain long-term financial stability, it is crucial to develop sound financial practices, such as budgeting, saving, and investing. People can take charge of their financial destiny and accomplish their goals by thinking back on their financial decisions and learning from their mistakes.

CHAPTER Ten

Giving back and donating money to charitable causes

Giving back and making financial contributions to charity organizations are firmly ingrained in the nation's cultural and religious traditions. Giving is viewed as a way to demonstrate thanks for blessings received and as a way to perform one's social responsibility to those in need in society.

Money can be donated to charity causes in India in a variety of ways by both private citizens and institutions. Direct donations to nonprofit organizations or NGOs (Non-Governmental Organizations) that support diverse causes like environmental preservation, healthcare, education, and poverty alleviation are one popular way to raise money. These organizations frequently have a significant presence in the neighborhood and aim to empower marginalized populations and develop long-term fixes for social and environmental problems.

Through religious organizations like mosques, gurudwaras, and temples is another common way to give money in India. These organizations receive a lot of monetary donations, which they subsequently utilize to support a range of charitable and religious endeavors like giving the poor food and shelter, setting up medical clinics, and holding religious rituals.

Online donation platforms have grown in popularity in India over the past few years. These platforms enable people and organizations to give money from the convenience of their homes to a variety of philanthropic causes. Many of these platforms also offer accountability and transparency by regularly updating users on how donations are being used.

Donating money to charitable causes in India has a number of tax advantages as well. The government has developed a number of programmes that offer tax deductions for donations given to various charitable purposes, such as the National Relief Fund and the Prime Minister's National Relief Fund.

In general, giving back and making financial contributions to charity organizations are deeply ingrained in Indian culture and society. It is regarded as a means of fulfilling one's social obligation to the less fortunate members of society and of fostering a more equitable and just society.

India offers a wide range of philanthropic causes to which people and organizations can contribute money, including:

Education: Numerous organizations in India seek to increase disadvantaged children's access to education. Donating money to these groups can assist with building schools and classrooms, providing educational resources, and funding scholarships.

Healthcare: Donating money to NGOs and healthcare groups can assist in giving those in need access to care and support. This can involve providing money for clinics, hospitals, and medical camps in addition to aiding in the creation of fresh medications and treatments.

Poverty alleviation: In India, poverty is still a significant problem, and numerous organizations are dedicated to reducing it and enhancing the lives of people who are less fortunate. Donating money to these organizations can assist in meeting the fundamental needs of people living in poverty, such as food, housing, and other essentials.

Environmental conservation: Environmental conservation has grown in importance as a result of India's economy and population's fast growth. Donating money to groups that promote environmental sustainability and conservation can support projects like reforestation, wildlife preservation, and the development of renewable energy sources.

Disaster relief: Natural calamities like cyclones, earthquakes, and floods are common in India. Donating money to disaster relief organizations can aid those affected by these occurrences by providing resources and support.

These are just a few examples of the types of charities that people and organizations in India can support financially. There are many more options for organizations and causes, so it's critical to conduct your homework and select one that is in line with your priorities and values.

CHAPTER Eleven

Recognising the function of banks and other financial organizations in controlling finances

Banks and other financial organizations are essential to the management of finances.

They offer a wide range of financial services to private citizens, corporate clients, and governmental organizations.

Deposits, loans, investments, and foreign exchange services are a few of the important services provided by banks and financial institutions.

Deposits: Deposits from both individuals and companies are accepted by banks and other financial organizations. Savings accounts, fixed deposits, recurring deposits, and current accounts are all possible forms of these deposits. These deposits assist banks in financing their lending operations.

Loans: Banks and financial organizations provide a range of loans, including business, personal, housing, and auto loans. Based on their creditworthiness and ability to repay the loan, these loans are granted to people and businesses. These loans have different interest rates depending on the loan type and the borrower's creditworthiness.

Investments: Additionally, banks and other financial institutions provide investment services such as stocks, bonds, and mutual funds. These investments support long-term wealth growth for both individuals and companies. In order to assist their clients in making wise investment decisions, banks also provide investment advising services.

Foreign exchange services: Banks and financial institutions further provide both private and commercial customers with foreign exchange services. These services consist of wire transfers, currency exchange, and foreign currency accounts. Businesses who need to conduct worldwide commerce will find these services to be very helpful.

Along with providing these essential services, banks and other financial institutions are crucial to controlling the amount of money in the economy. By regulating interest rates and the amount of credit accessible in the economy, they are able to do this. India's central bank, the Reserve Bank of India (RBI), is in charge of overseeing banking regulations and controlling the nation's money supply.

In conclusion, banks and other financial institutions play a crucial role in the economy. They assist in controlling the money supply, offer a range of financial services to people and businesses, and promote economic expansion.

Here are some examples of banks and financial institutions in India:

One of the biggest public sector banks in India, State Bank of India offers both people and companies a comprehensive range of banking services.

ICICI Bank is a private sector bank that provides its clients with banking, credit, investment, and insurance services.

Another private sector bank that offers loans, investments, and banking services to people and businesses is HDFC Bank.

Axis Bank is a private sector bank that provides its clients with a range of banking services, loans, and investment services.

A public sector bank, Punjab National Bank offers both individuals and companies a variety of banking, credit, and investment services.

Bajaj Finserv is a non-banking financial institution (NBFI) that provides its clients with a variety of financial services, such as loans, investments, and insurance services.

A subsidiary of the Life Insurance Corporation of India, LIC Housing Finance Limited offers house loans to private customers for the purchase or construction of dwellings.

These are but a few illustrations of the banks and financial organizations present in India. In India, there are many more banks and financial institutions that provide both private citizens and commercial clients with a range of financial services.

CHAPTER Twelve

Knowledge of inflation and how it affects the value of money

Over time, inflation is defined as a rise in the average level of prices for goods and services. The Consumer Price Index (CPI), which records the price fluctuations of a basket of products and services frequently used by households, is used in India to measure inflation.

People can buy less with the same amount of money when inflation is strong because the value of money declines.

There are several ways to view how inflation affects the value of money in India:

Purchasing power: Money loses some of its purchasing value when inflation is strong. As a result, people can spend the same amount of money on fewer goods and services. A commodity that costs Rs. 100 today will cost Rs. 105 next year, for instance, if inflation is 5%. This implies that in the future, a given amount of money will buy less products and services.

Interest rates: Interest rates may rise as a result of high inflation rates. To combat the effects of inflation, banks and other financial institutions may raise the interest rates on loans and fixed deposits. This may have an effect on how people and companies in the economy borrow and lend money.

Wages: Employee earnings may be impacted by inflation. Employees may seek higher pay as the cost of living rises as a result of inflation in order to maintain their level of life. This might raise the cost of production for companies, which would ultimately result in higher prices for goods and services.

Foreign trade: A nation's foreign trade may be impacted by inflation. The value of the Indian rupee may fall in relation to other currencies if India's inflation rate is higher than that of other nations. This might result in less demand for Indian exports and more demand for imports, which would result in a trade deficit.

Inflation control in the economy is the responsibility of the Reserve Bank of India (RBI). In order to manage inflation, it makes use of a variety of monetary policy measures, including interest rates, reserve requirements, and open market operations. In order to limit inflation, the government also implements policies including restricting access to basic commodities and services, providing subsidies, and setting price controls.

As it affects the value of money, purchasing power, interest rates, wages, and international trade, inflation is a crucial economic term in India. In order to keep prices stable and under control, the government and the RBI take action.

To demonstrate how inflation affects the value of money, consider the following example:

Let's assume that India experiences 5% annual inflation. This means that due to inflation, a good that costs Rs. 100 now will cost Rs. 105 in a year. As a result, 100 rupees will have less purchasing power the following year since they can buy fewer goods and services.

For instance, if a person spends Rs. 10,000 per month and the inflation rate is 5%, they will require Rs. 10,500 the next year to maintain the same quality of life. This is related to inflation, which makes a given amount of money able to purchase fewer products and services.

The real value of an individual's account will diminish over time if they have a fixed deposit of Rs. 1 lakh with a bank and the inflation rate is 5%. The nominal value of the deposit stays the same, but inflation reduces the money's purchasing power. This indicates that, in actual terms, the deposit's value is declining and that, for the same amount of money, the individual may purchase fewer products and services.

As a result, there are many areas of the Indian economy where inflation has an impact on the value of money, and it is crucial that individuals, companies, and the government take action to control inflation and maintain price stability.

CHAPTER Thirteen

Taking Control of Financial Stress and Anxiety

In this chapter, we examine the particular financial challenges that students frequently experience and offer doable management and coping mechanisms. Students can take charge of their finances and improve their general well-being by comprehending the causes of financial stress, putting stress-reduction strategies into practice, getting professional support when necessary, and developing resilience.

Section 1: Determine the Causes of Financial Stress

1.1 Educational Costs and Tuition:

Students and their families are under financial strain as a result of India's rising cost of education.

Solution: To manage their tuition costs and educational expenses, students can look into scholarships, grants, part-time jobs, or educational loans. They can proactively look for scholarships and grants that fit their qualifications and financial circumstances and apply for them. Taking on part-time work or an internship can help you make extra money. If necessary, student loans can be taken into consideration, but it's crucial to be aware of the terms and conditions before choosing this option.

1.2 Peer Pressure and Expectations Regarding Lifestyle:

Students' purchasing patterns are influenced by peer pressure as they try to live up to social expectations.

Solution: Students should make informed financial decisions and distinguish between needs and wants. Prioritize vital expenditures and cut back on frivolous spending. Students can avoid the temptation to splurge in order to live up to peer expectations by staying true to their principles and financial goals. Case studies of students who have successfully managed their financial obligations while upholding their ideals can serve as an example and a source of motivation.

Section 2: Implementing Stress-Reduction Techniques.

2.1 Financial planning and budgeting:

I am focusing on the Budget from the start of the book because everything will depend on this only.

Budgeting is a method for keeping track of earnings, costs, and savings.

By noting their sources of income and classifying their expenses (such as schooling, housing, food, and transportation), students can build a budget. They should set aside money for the most important expenses first. Making sensible financial decisions and saving money may be achieved by following simple advice like comparison shopping, meal planning, and taking advantage of student discounts.

2.2 Self-Care and Mindfulness:

Managing stress is crucial since financial stress has an impact on overall wellbeing.

Solutions: To lessen worry due to their financial position, students should practice mindfulness techniques like meditation or deep breathing exercises. Exercise, hobbies, and quality family time are all examples of self-care activities that can help you keep a positive outlook even when things are difficult.

Section 3: Professional Assistance When Needed

3.1 Student Support Services and Financial Counseling:

Financial counseling services are provided by external organizations and educational institutions.

The best way for students to seek financial counseling services is to be aware of their availability. The creation of a financial plan can be aided by seeking professional help, which can offer personalized guidance. Stories of students who have benefited from these programmes and overcame obstacles to their financial well-being can serve as an example for others.

3.2 Manage Debt and Repaying Loans

Credit card debt and other forms of accumulated debt can be distressing.

Solutions: Students can look into debt management choices including consolidating loans, negotiating repayment conditions, or getting help from an expert. It's critical to examine governmental efforts or loan forgiveness programmes, such as income-based repayment plans, that provide support for loan payback.

Section 4: Build Resilience and a Sense of Control.

4.1 Increasing Financial Intelligence:

Students get the ability to make wise judgements through financial education.

Students should prioritize raising their level of financial literacy. They can learn about personal finance by utilizing resources like books, online, or workshops. Students can develop confidence in efficiently managing their finances by learning about budgeting, saving, investing, and managing credit.

4.2 Established a Helpful Network:

Having a strong support system nearby is helpful while facing financial difficulties.

Solutions: Students should be honest about their financial struggles with friends, family, and role models. Insights and support can be gained by asking individuals who have successfully handled comparable circumstances for advice.

Students can successfully manage their financial stress and anxiety by putting the techniques described in this chapter into practice. They may take charge of their finances, lessen stress via mindfulness and budgeting, seek expert assistance when necessary, and develop resilience. Students may confidently navigate their financial path and concentrate on their personal and academic success by making deliberate financial decisions, developing financial literacy, and looking for help from a network.

Now, It's time to give a practical example to connect you with the topic.

So, Let's Meet Rajesh, a college student. Due to the rising cost of education and peer pressure to maintain a certain lifestyle, Rajesh is experiencing financial stress and worry.

Here is how Rajesh manages his financial stress using the techniques covered in the chapter:

Identifying Sources of Financial Stress, Rajesh looks into and submits applications for grants and scholarships to help down his tuition fees and educational costs.

In order to supplement his income and pay for a portion of his living expenses, he accepts a part-time position on campus.

Putting Stress-Reduction Techniques into Practice

Rajesh develops a monthly budget to keep track of his earnings and outlays. While dedicating a percentage of his income to savings, he prioritizes necessities like tuition, housing, and food.

To reduce worry due to his financial circumstances, he uses mindfulness techniques including meditation and deep breathing exercises.

When necessary, Rajesh seeks professional assistance; he makes use of the college's financial counseling programme. He meets with a financial counselor, who offers advice on managing his student debts and helpful ideas for debt reduction while also assisting him in developing a personalized financial plan.

Building Resilience and a Sense of Control: Rajesh reads books and attends workshops on personal finance at the advice of his financial advisor. He gains confidence and financial understanding as a result of doing this.

He enrolls in a student support group where he can speak honestly about his financial difficulties and get help from other students who have faced and overcome similar circumstances.

Rajesh is able to properly manage his financial stress and anxiety by putting these ideas into practice. He is able to concentrate on his studies without continual stress because he feels like he has more control over his finances. Rajesh is able to handle his financial journey with resiliency and confidence thanks to his proactive attitude and the resources and help at his disposal.

CHAPTER Fourteen

Saving Money

This chapter could provide tips on how to save money, including how to set up a savings account, how to make automatic transfers, and how to use coupons.

Saving money is now essential for future planning and financial stability in the fast-paced world we live in. Let's first examine the idea of saving money and its significance in the Indian setting, then go on to real-world examples that provide helpful advice for efficient saving tactics.

Section 1: Understanding the Value of Saving Money.

1.1 The Idea of Saving Cash

Setting aside a portion of one's salary for future usage or crises is referred to as saving money. To meet objectives, deal with unforeseen costs, and attain long-term financial security, it entails building a financial cushion.

1.2 India's Economic Challenges

The Indian economy has particular difficulties, including escalating inflation, growing living expenses, and volatile market conditions. Due to these aspects, saving money is even more crucial for those who want to overcome financial obstacles and accomplish their goals.

1.3 Advantages of Saving Cash

Numerous advantages come from saving money, including:

Building money: People can build money over time and become financially independent by persistently saving and investing.

Goal Attained: Saving money assists people in making plans for significant life events like purchasing a home, starting a family, or going to college.

Emergency Fund: Having a savings cushion offers protection from unforeseen events like job loss or medical emergency.

1.4 A Cultural View of Saving:

Saving money is highly ingrained in Indian cultural beliefs.

People in India learn the value of saving money and respecting tradition while modifying it to meet current financial goals by watching how their parents and grandparents save money for festivals, weddings, and other major occasions.

An illustration is Ravi, a young Indian professional, who sees his parents setting aside money for his sister's wedding. Inspired by their dedication to monetary stability, Ravi makes the decision to start saving in order to secure a secure future for himself.

Section 2: Setting Up a Savings Account.

2.1 Selecting the Correct Bank:

The correct bank must be chosen if you want to begin saving efficiently. Reputation, accessibility, costs, interest rates, and customer service are all important considerations. People can make an informed choice by investigating various Indian banks.

As an illustration, Ravi thoroughly investigates various banks and contrasts their services. He chooses a bank that meets his demands after taking into account elements like minimum balance requirements, interest rates, and online banking capabilities.

2.2 Different Savings Account Types:

It is easier to select the best option for a person if they are aware of the many sorts of savings accounts available in India. There are other possibilities, including standard savings accounts, high-interest savings accounts, and specialized accounts for certain objectives like retirement or education.

As an illustration, Ravi examines the attributes of various types of savings accounts. He carefully considers his options and decides to maximize his savings potential by opening a high-interest savings account.

2.3 Opening an Account for Savings:

People must adhere to the bank's account creation procedures, provide the necessary papers, and read and comprehend the account terms and conditions in order to open a savings account.

Example: Ravi visits the bank of his choice, sets up the account, and makes sure he is familiar with all of the account's features.

Section 3: Making Automatic Transfers.

3.1 Recognising Automatic Transfers:

Automatic transfers are a practical approach to routinely save money. People can plan for a certain amount to be sent from their checking account to their savings account at regular intervals by setting up automatic transfers.

As an illustration, Ravi discovers automatic transfers and recognises their potential to assist him in continuously saving money. In order to automatically transfer a specific amount from his checking account to his savings account each month, he decides to set up automatic transfers.

3.2 Choosing Savings Objectives:

To keep motivated and focused, it's imperative to set realistic savings objectives. To estimate how much they can comfortably save each month, people must evaluate their income, spending, and debt obligations.

Ravi, for instance, has clear objectives for his savings, such as setting aside a certain portion of his pay each month and achieving a certain amount by a certain date. To efficiently monitor his progress, he divides his goals into more manageable milestones.

3.3 Bill Payment Automation:

The elimination of late fees and penalties is ensured by automating bill payments. People can focus on their savings goals by freeing up mental spacc by setting up automatic bill payments.

For instance, Ravi is aware of the value of automating bill payments to prevent late fines. In order to ensure that his bills are paid on time and without any human effort, he enrolls in automated bill payment services offered by his bank or utility companies.

Section 4: Using Discounts and Coupons.

4.1 Online discounts and couponing

People now have access to a variety of couponing strategies and internet resources that provide savings on groceries, dining out, entertainment, and other regular expenses. Comparison websites, discount codes, and coupon applications are all useful tools.

For instance, Ravi researches couponing strategies and finds websites and apps that offer deals on groceries and meals. He begins to use these tools to make purchases while saving money, eventually releasing large savings.

4.2 Strategic Purchases and Smart Shopping:

Making a shopping list, comparing costs, and avoiding impulse buys are all wise shopping practices that help you save money. Purchasing non-perishable goods or necessities in bulk can also result in cost savings and discounts.

As an illustration, Ravi establishes the practice of compiling a shopping list and comparing pricing at various retailers before making a purchase. Additionally, he starts stocking up on non-perishable goods in bulk to take advantage of sales and save costs all around.

Section 5: Managing Obstacles and Maintaining Savings Habits

5.1 Changing Your Lifestyle:

Savings habits can be impacted by life events and shifting circumstances. When faced with promotions, moves, or the beginnings of a family, people need to reevaluate their spending plans and savings objectives. It's essential to adapt to new circumstances while continuing to save money.

Example: Ravi receives a promotion and sees an increase in his earnings. While acknowledging this accomplishment, he reviews his spending plan, modifies his savings objectives, and makes sure that he continues to save aside a sizable amount of his new income.

5.2 Monitoring Development and Honoring Milestones:

Regularly monitoring savings progress and marking achievements encourages saving behavior. To successfully measure their progress, people can utilize budgeting apps, spreadsheets, or specific savings trackers.

As an illustration, Ravi maintains track of his savings and recognises progress along the way. He gives himself a tiny incentive, like a nice meal or a day trip, when he meets a set savings goal or eliminates a big debt.

We have looked at useful advice for cost-cutting in the Indian environment using Ravi as an actual-life example. The first steps to financial security include realizing the value of saving, opening a savings account, setting up automated transfers, and taking advantage of coupons and discounts. People like Ravi may build and maintain good saving habits, safeguarding their financial future and reaching their goals, by overcoming obstacles, monitoring progress, and seeking support. Saving money is a lifestyle decision that contributes to a future that is more secure and happy rather than merely a financial practice.

CHAPTER

Fifteen

Managing finances in relationships

Relationships and money are intertwined, and sound financial management is essential to a happy marriage. This chapter will cover useful techniques for handling money in relationships, such as clear communication, setting mutual financial objectives, handling joint finances, and settling arguments. We will provide practical examples to show how couples may build a strong financial foundation and deepen their relationship.

Section 1: Open Communication Regarding Money

1.1 The Value of Honest Communication

A solid financial partnership is built on open and honest communication regarding finances. To build trust and understanding, it entails talking about each person's financial circumstances, views, anxieties, and objectives.

As an illustration, newlyweds Priya and Rohit place a high value on candid financial communication. They organize "money talks" on a regular basis where they discuss their earnings, outgoings, and financial goals, promoting openness and harmony in their union.

1.2 Sharing Financial Histories

Couples can better understand one another's financial backgrounds by discussing their own financial histories, including their debts, assets, and spending patterns. Finding common ground and cultivating empathy are made easier with this information.

Aman and Neha, a couple who intend to combine their finances, reveal their financial backgrounds. Neha shows her savings and investment portfolio, while Aman discloses his student loan burden. They can make wise judgments as a pair if they are aware of each other's financial conditions.

1.3 Talking about values and financial goals

Couples' aspirations can be aligned and a roadmap for their financial journey can be created by talking about shared financial goals and values. It entails talking about both immediate and long-term objectives, like starting a family, saving for retirement, or purchasing a home.

When Suresh and Meera talk about their financial objectives, they discover that they both place a high value on trip experiences. They create a savings strategy specifically for travel, giving their mutual aspirations top priority in terms of money.

Section 2: Establishing Shared Financial Goals and Values.

2.1 Determining Shared Objectives

Couples can cooperate to achieve mutual goals by identifying shared financial goals. It entails talking about aims, establishing priorities, and figuring out the procedures necessary to reach those objectives.

For instance, Ravi and Shreya sit down to discuss their financial objectives. They learn that they both wish to start early retirement plans and save for their child's school. They can align their financial choices by identifying their shared objectives.

2.2 Setting Individual Aspirations in Priority:

While recognising and respecting individual aspirations is key, achieving shared goals is as necessary. Couples should talk about and figure out strategies to support one another's financial goals.

As an illustration, Aarti wants to open her own business, whilst Sameer wants to continue his education. Along with their common objectives, they give individual dreams equal weight, investing finances and resources to assist one another's projects.

2.3 Making a Financial Roadmap

Setting deadlines, measuring progress, and breaking down goals into manageable segments are all part of creating a financial plan. With the help of this road plan, couples may stay motivated and focused as they progress towards financial success.

As an illustration, Arjun and Ananya create a financial plan to help them save money for a down payment on a home. They decide on a monthly savings goal, look into several types of mortgages, and routinely assess their progress. This road map aids them in staying on course and completing their homeownership objective.

Section 3: Managing Joint Financials and Individual Responsibilities

3.1 Integrating Finances:

For many couples, combining funds is a big step. It entails combining bank accounts, creating shared budgeting platforms, and allocating financial duties.

Example: After getting married, Karan and Nisha wish to combine their finances. They establish a collective budget and open a joint bank account to manage their shared costs, assuring openness and cooperation.

3.2 Determining Each Person's Responsibilities:

Couples can take use of their particular strengths and preserve their sense of self by dividing financial obligations. Depending on their preferences and abilities, they can assign responsibilities like managing investments, maintaining the budget, or paying bills.

Example: Riya overseas long-term investments, whereas Deepak is in charge of paying bills on time each month and keeping track of spending. They can make use of their individual skills and collaborate effectively thanks to the division of labor.

3.3 Setting Financial Boundaries and Spending Limits:

Couples can maintain financial stability and prevent needless arguments by creating financial boundaries and spending restrictions. It entails talking about discretionary spending, establishing appropriate spending limits, and respecting one another's financial restrictions.

For instance, Rajiv and Shalini set spending caps for luxuries like dining out and shopping. To encourage financial accountability and prevent surprises, they agree to contact one another before making large purchases.

Section 4: Resolving Conflicts and Reaching Financial Compromises

4.1 Resolving Conflicts Peacefully:

Conflicts about money can arise in relationships. It's critical to resolve disputes amicably by hearing each other out, expressing your concerns, and coming up with solutions that benefit all parties.

Example: Vikram and Deepika occasionally argue because of their distinct spending styles. They actively listen to one another, consider each other's points of view, and reach agreements that satisfy everyone's requirements while preserving their financial harmony.

4.2 Seeking Expert Assistance:

To resolve complex financial problems, it may occasionally be helpful to seek professional assistance, such as couples therapy or financial counseling. Professionals can offer advice, mediate arguments, and suggest ways to settle disputes.

For instance, Ritu and Sunil's relationship is strained by ongoing financial disputes. They enlist the aid of a financial counselor, who works with them to resolve their financial arguments by assisting them in identifying underlying problems, enhancing communication, and finding workable solutions.

4.3 Finding Compromises

When a couple has different financial interests or strategies, finding compromises is essential. It calls for flexibility, a desire to comprehend one another's viewpoints, and the exploration of original ideas that can satisfy the demands of both partners.

Example: While Rahul wants unplanned encounters, Maya prefers to save for the future. By allocating money for both long-term savings and sporadic impulsive experiences, they reach a compromise that satisfies both of their needs.

Open communication, common financial objectives, efficient management of joint finances, and the capacity for dispute resolution are all necessary for navigating money in relationships. We have looked at how couples can set shared financial goals, manage joint finances, and reach compromises through examples from real-life relationships. Couples can improve their relationship, create financial harmony, and work towards a wealthy future by putting these suggestions into practice. Keep in mind that managing your finances is a process that calls for trust, understanding, and assistance from others.

CHAPTER Sixteen

How to Develop a Prosperity Mindset

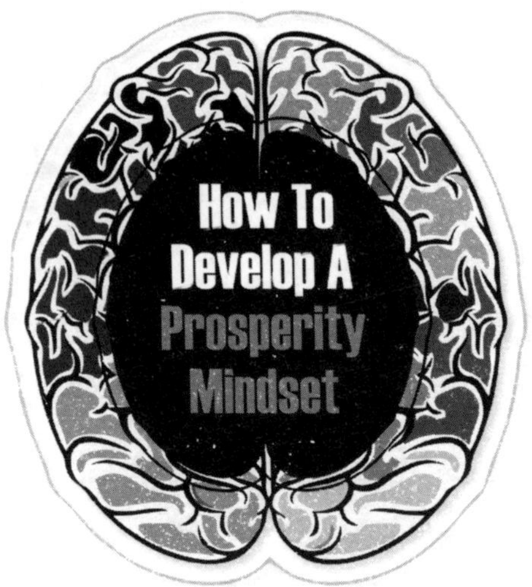

This chapter will examine the idea of developing a prosperity mindset and practical methods for changing from a mindset of scarcity to one of abundance. People can reach their full potential for financial abundance by cultivating gratitude, dispelling limiting attitudes about money, and adopting a positive outlook on wealth development. We will show how adopting a prosperity mentality can result in good improvements in one's financial journey through accessible examples and doable methods.

Section 1: Moving from Scarcity to Abundance Thinking.

The foundation of scarcity thinking is the idea that there is a finite quantity of wealth, opportunity, and resources available. On the other hand, abundance thinking is predicated on the notion that the world is full of resources and opportunity. It is essential to make the switch from scarcity to abundance thinking in order to develop a prosperity mindset.

Case in point: Sarah

Young professional Sarah had always had trouble with the concept of scarcity. She thought that opportunities were few and that there was never enough money to satisfy her desires. She made the decision to oppose this way of thinking, though, and began concentrating on abundance. She reminded herself that there are countless opportunities in the world and that she has the ability to make money on her own. Sarah's perspective changed, and she started looking for ways to improve herself and succeed financially.

Section 2: Practice Gratitude and Appreciation.

One of the most effective methods for developing a prosperity mindset is thankfulness practice. It entails being aware of and grateful for the riches and gifts already present in one's life. You may attract more into your life by being grateful for what you already have and acknowledging it.

The journey of Mark, for instance.

A middle-aged professional named Mark came to the realization that his continual attention on what he lacked caused him to frequently ignore the benefits in his life. He made the decision to begin a thankfulness practice by listing three things every day. He expressed gratitude for his opportunities, his healthy state, and his loving family. Mark observed a noticeable mental shift as he continued this practice. He started attracting more wealth into his life and started feeling happier with his existing financial condition.

Section 3: Dispelling Money-Related Limiting Beliefs

Money-related limiting ideas can prevent people from obtaining financial success. These opinions are frequently the result of prior encounters, social training, or destructive self-talk. It's crucial to recognise and get rid of these limiting attitudes if you want to develop a prosperity mindset.

Samantha's Transformation, for instance

Samantha came from a family where money was always tight. She thereby formed the limiting conviction that she would never be financially secure. Samantha was aware, though, that this notion was preventing her from realizing her full potential. She asked for assistance from a financial coach, who led her through a process of questioning and paraphrasing her limiting ideas. Samantha eventually overcame her unhelpful beliefs and replaced them with empowering ones like "I am capable of creating abundance" and "Money flows easily to me." As a result, Samantha's perspective changed, and she started to draw in more possibilities and money.

Section 4: Embracing a Positive Outlook on Wealth Creation.

Wealth accumulation is not always bad or self-serving. It is a way of thinking that accepts the possibility of development, achievement, and financial prosperity. People who have a positive perspective on wealth development can see money as a tool for making a positive difference and finding personal fulfillment.

Example: James's Story

James, a social entrepreneur, had a bad opinion of money creation from the beginning. He connected it to consumerism and greed. But as James thought more deeply about his mission and his desire to change the world, he saw that making money might be a way to go where he wanted to go. He adopted a constructive perspective on wealth accumulation because he understood that if he had enough money, he could have a bigger impact on the things he was passionate about. James established a prosperous company that not only brought him cash but also enabled him to make a difference in his neighborhood.

A prosperous mindset can be attained, but it takes conscious work and introspection to do so. We have learned from Sarah, Mark, Samantha, and James's experiences how people may change their perspective from one of scarcity to one of plenty, cultivate thankfulness and appreciation, get rid of limiting notions about money, and adopt a constructive outlook on wealth building. These real-world examples show that anyone can develop a prosperity mentality and realize their true financial potential. People can have a fruitful connection with money by implementing these tactics into their lives, which will increase their financial success, sense of fulfillment, and outlook on the future.

CHAPTER Seventeen

Now, it's time to learn some finance thumb rules that will help you manage your finances.

A well-liked budgeting principle that can assist people in allocating their cash properly is the 50/30/20 rule. It advises allocating 50% of your post-tax income for needs, 30% for wants, and 20% for savings and debt repayment. To show how this rule might be used in practice, let's examine each category and offer real-world examples.

1. 50% for Needs: Expenses that are necessary for daily living go under the needs category. This covers accommodation,

utilities, travel, shopping, health care, and the bare minimum of debt payments.

Let's dissect each element and offer real-world examples:

a.) **Housing:** Set aside some of your money for rent or mortgage payments, real estate taxes, and homeowner's insurance. If your monthly income is Rs. 2,000, for example, you should aim to spend no more than Rs. 1,000 on housing-related costs.

b.) Include expenses for power, water, heating, internet, and phone bills under the heading "Utilities." Calculate these expenditures based on your typical monthly usage, and give energy-saving techniques top priority to reduce costs.

c.) **Transportation:** Include costs for driving, taking public transportation, paying for a car, petrol, insurance, and upkeep. Make sure your Rs. 200 monthly transportation-related spending is within the 50% allowance, for instance.

d.) **Groceries:** Create a plan and budget for your food costs, including groceries, meal planning, and eating in. Think about using coupons, buying at deals, and choosing affordable lunch options.

e.) **Healthcare:** Set aside money for prescription costs, co-pays, and other medical expenses. Make sure your Rs. 100 monthly healthcare expenses fall below the 50% range.

f.) **Minimum Debt Payments:** Include any necessary

debt repayments, such as credit card minimum payments or school loan repayments. When possible, try to make extra payments towards debt to hasten the process of paying it off.

2. **30% for Wants:** Expenses that are optional but nevertheless improve your lifestyle but are not necessary for survival are included in the wants category. This can include a variety of entertainment options, dining out, travel, and hobbies. Here are some real-world examples:

    a.) **Entertainment:** Set aside money for things like attending sporting events, concerts, and movies. Make sure your Rs. 100 monthly entertainment budget stays under the 30% allotment.

    b.) **Dining Out:** Set aside money for occasional treats, takeaway and meals at restaurants. For instance, the Rs. 150 you budget each month for eating out should fall within the 30% area.

    c.) **Vacations:** Save money for trips and other fun activities. To stay within the allotted 30% of your salary for travel, it's crucial to budget and save in advance.

    d.) **Hobbies:** Set aside money for your passions in things like sports, crafts, or musical instruments. Make sure your Rs. 50 monthly hobby expenses fit within the 30% limit, for instance.

3. **20% for Savings and Debt Repayment:** This category is essential for establishing financial stability and lowering

debt. It entails putting money aside for retirement, investments, and debt repayment over and beyond the required minimum payments. Here are some real-world examples:

a.) Create an emergency fund by allocating a percentage of your income in this direction. Save enough money to cover three to six months' worth of expenses in order to have a safety net in case of unforeseen financial circumstances.

b.) **Retirement Savings:** Make contributions to IRAs and 401(k)s, among other retirement accounts. Make the most of any matching contributions provided by your employer to increase your retirement savings.

c.) **Investments:** To increase your wealth over time, think about investing a percentage of your income in stocks, bonds, or mutual funds. Consult the ideal investment solutions for your objectives with a financial advisor.

d.) **Additional Debt Payments:** Set aside money above and beyond the required minimum payments to hasten the repayment of debt. To reduce future interest costs, prioritize paying off high-interest debts first, such as credit cards and private education loans.

Practical illustration

Let's think about the following situation:

Monthly earnings after taxes: Rs. 3,000

50 percent for needs

1,000 (Rs. 33.33 percent of income) for housing

- Rs. 200 (6.67% of income) is spent on utilities.

- Travel: Rs. 300 (or 10% of salary)

- Food: Rs. 250, or 8.33% of income

- Medical costs: Rs. 100 (3.33% of income).

- Rs. 200 monthly minimum payment on debt (6.67% of income)

30 percent for wants:

- Recreation: Rs. 150 (5% of income)

- Rs. 200 (Rs. 6.67% of income) for eating out

- Rs. 100 for vacations (3.33% of income)

- Interests: Rs. 50 (1.67% of gross income)

20% for Debt Repayment and Savings:

- Rs. 300 for an emergency fund (10% of income)

- Savings for retirement: Rs. 200 (6.67% of income)

- Rs. 100 in investments (3.33% of income)

- Rs. 150 (5% of income) in additional debt payments

In this case, the person is using the 50/30/20 rule to distribute their money. The percentages given are rough estimates based on a monthly salary of Rs. 3,000 alone. On the basis of unique circumstances and priorities, adjustments can be made.

By adhering to the 50/30/20 rule, people can keep a balanced budget, pay for necessities, indulge in discretionary spending, and give savings and debt reduction priority. It offers a well-organized framework to support people in successfully managing their money and achieving their financial objectives.

Keep in mind that personal money is very individualized, so it's crucial to customize the budgeting principles to your own needs and objectives. To make sure that your budget reflects the changes in your financial status, examine and reevaluate it frequently.

Emergency Fund

An essential component of personal finance is having an emergency fund. It serves as a safety net for your finances, giving you comfort and security through unforeseen circumstances that may otherwise put a heavy strain on your finances. In this section, we'll go in-depth on the value of an emergency fund, talk about its ideal size, and give a real-world example to highlight its usefulness.

1. The Value of Having an Emergency Fund: An emergency fund is a collection of funds set aside, particularly to deal with unforeseen costs or other financial catastrophes. It acts as a safety net, enabling you to deal with unforeseen circumstances without turning to high-interest loans or using up all of your long-term resources. The following details highlight the necessity of an emergency fund:

    a.) **Job Loss:** Having an emergency fund might give you a financial safety net to pay your living expenses while you look for new employment in the event of a sudden job loss.

b.) **Medical Emergencies:** Unexpected medical costs might be high and put a burden on your finances. Unexpected medical charges or other expenses might be paid for with the use of an emergency fund.

c.) Home repairs may be expensive, whether the problem is a leaking roof, a malfunctioning appliance, or a plumbing problem. Having an emergency reserve guarantees that you can cover these costs without going over budget.

d.) **Auto Repairs:** Problems with vehicles can occur at any time, and repairs can be pricey. If you have an emergency fund, you can pay for these costs without interfering with your regular routine or taking out expensive loans.

e.) **Unexpected Travel:** On occasion, a family emergency or other pressing circumstances may require you to travel immediately. The money required to pay for travel expenses may be available from an emergency reserve.

f.) **Unforeseen Events:** Because life is unpredictable, it is possible for accidents, natural disasters, and legal issues to occur. The financial means to deal with these circumstances are provided by an emergency fund.

Debt to Income Ratio

The Debt-to-Income Ratio (DTI) is a vital financial metric that lenders and consumers use to determine a person's capacity to handle debt. The ratio of a person's monthly debt payments to their monthly income is measured. Maintaining a sound financial profile requires awareness of and attention to your DTI ratio. We will examine the significance of the DTI ratio in this part, as well as how to calculate it and use a real-world example to do so.

The Debt-to-Income Ratio's Importance

When determining a borrower's creditworthiness, lenders often base their decision on the DTI ratio. It gives information about a person's capacity to balance their present debt obligations with their income. The DTI ratio is significant for the following main reasons:

a.) Loan Eligibility: Lenders utilize the DTI ratio to assess a borrower's suitability for several loans, including personal, vehicle, and home loans. A borrower that has a low DTI ratio has less debt in relation to their income, increasing their chance of loan approval.

b.) Financial Stability: A lower DTI ratio indicates better financial stability because it shows that less of the household's income is going towards paying off debt. This suggests a reduced danger of default and a higher probability of continuing sound financial practices.

c.) Budgeting and Debt Management: Determining your DTI ratio gives you important information about your present debt load and aids in your assessment of your capacity to handle debt. Based on your salary, it acts as a benchmark to determine whether you have a tolerable level of debt.

d.) Financial Planning: By tracking your DTI ratio over time, you can see how much debt you have paid off and how your financial situation has improved. It aids in your decision-making while deciding whether to take on additional debt or change your debt repayment plan.

How to Determine Your Debt-to-Income Ratio

You must know your entire monthly debt payments as well as your gross monthly income in order to calculate your DTI ratio. To determine your DTI ratio, take the following actions:

a.) Calculate Your Monthly Total Debt Payments: Add up all of your regular monthly debt payments, including credit card bills, vehicle loans, student loans, personal loans, mortgage or rent, and any other regular monthly debts.

b.) Determine Your Gross Monthly Income: Determine your gross monthly income, which includes all of your pre-tax income from jobs, bonuses, commissions, rental income, and other sources.

c.) Divide entire Monthly Debt Payments by Gross Monthly Income: To calculate your DTI ratio, divide the entire monthly debt payments by the gross monthly income. The result is multiplied by 100.

The DTI ratio calculation formula is as follows:

Total Monthly Debt Payments / Gross Monthly Income multiplied by 100 is the DTI Ratio.

Consider Alex as an illustration. He makes the following monthly loan payments and has the following gross monthly income:

Debt payments per month:

Rs. 200 monthly mortgage payment

Payment on Auto Loan: Rs. 300

Payment for Student Loans: Rs. 200

Payments with credit card: Rs. 100

Monthly debt payments total Rs. 1,200 plus Rs. 300 plus Rs. 200 plus Rs. 100, or Rs. 1,800.

Rs. 4,500 is the monthly gross income.

Let's now determine Alex's DTI ratio:

DTI Ratio is equal to (Rs. 1,800/Rs. 4,500) × 100, or 40%.

The DTI ratio for Alex is 40%, meaning that 40% of his total monthly income is used to pay off debt.

Debt-to-Income Ratio Interpretation:

Understanding how to interpret your DTI ratio after you've calculated it is crucial. A lower DTI ratio is typically regarded as better because it indicates that less of your income is going towards paying off debt. The common DTI ratio categories are shown below:

a.) DTI ratio of under 20% is regarded as desirable. It means that only a small portion of your salary goes towards paying off debt, leaving you with a sizable amount of extra cash.

b.) 20% to 36%: A DTI ratio of 20% to 36% is typically seen as desirable. It implies that a reasonable amount of your salary goes towards paying off debt while still having money left over for savings and other needs.

c.) DTI ratio of 37% to 42%: A DTI ratio of 37% to 42%

is regarded as reasonable. It means that a substantial percentage of your income is going towards paying off debt, which may leave you with less money to save or borrow.

d.) Greater than 43%: A DTI ratio greater than 43% is regarded as excessive and can be cause for concern. It implies that a significant amount of your income is used to pay off debt, leaving little opportunity for savings and raising the possibility of financial stress.

It's crucial to remember that these categories are meant to be basic suggestions and that the ideal DTI ratio may change based on a person's unique situation and financial objectives. For instance, a person with a higher salary might be able to comfortably handle a somewhat higher DTI ratio.

Consider Sarah, a recent college graduate, who is analyzing her DTI ratio to determine how her financial situation is doing. Sarah's gross monthly income and monthly debt payments are as follows:

Debt payments per month:

Rs. 300 for student loan repayment

Payment for Auto Loan: Rs. 200

Payment with credit card: Rs. 100

Monthly Debt Payments: Rs. 300, Rs. 200, and Rs. 100, for a total of Rs. 600.

Rs. 2,500 is the gross monthly income.

Let's now determine Sarah's DTI ratio:

DTI Ratio is equal to (600/2,500) × 100, or 24%.

Sarah's DTI ratio is 24 percent, which is within the favorable range. This suggests that she allocates a reasonable amount of her salary to debt repayment, leaving her with money to save and pursue other financial objectives.

Let's consider two fictitious events to put Sarah's DTI ratio into perspective:

Improved debt management is scenario one.

In order to lower her monthly debt payments, Sarah makes the decision to pay off her debts in full. Her new monthly debt payments are as follows after refinancing her student loan and paying off the remaining amount on her credit card:

Debt payments per month:

Payment for Student Loans: Rs. 200

Payment for Auto Loan: Rs. 200

Monthly Debt Payments: Rs. 200 plus Rs. 200 equals Rs. 400.

Recalculating Sarah's DTI ratio now:

DTI Ratio = (400/2,500) x 100 = 16 percent

Sarah's DTI ratio has dropped to 16% because of better debt management, which is an outstanding level. She now has greater financial flexibility and has successfully reduced her debt load, according to this.

Scenario 2: a higher debt burden

In a different situation, Sarah decides to finance a large purchase, such a home, in order to incur more debt. These are her new monthly debt payments:

Debt payments per month:

Rs. 300 for student loan repayment

Payment for Auto Loan: Rs. 200

Rs. 500 monthly mortgage payment

Monthly Debt Payments: Rs. 300, Rs. 200, Rs. 1,500, or Rs. 2,000 total

Recalculating Sarah's DTI ratio now:

(2,000/2,500) x 100 = 80% DTI Ratio

Sarah's DTI ratio has climbed to 80% due to the increasing debt load, which is considered high. This suggests that she spends a substantial part of her income on debt repayments, which leaves little room for savings and might put her under more financial difficulty.

These examples show how important it is to manage debt and keep a healthy DTI ratio for overall financial well-being. To make sure your DTI ratio stays within a healthy range, it's crucial to regularly assess and modify your debt repayment strategy.

Advice for Increasing DTI Ratio:

You can take the following actions to raise your DTI ratio if it is higher than you would like it to be:

a.) Increase your income by, for example, asking for a raise, taking on a second job or freelance work, or obtaining more education or certifications that may open up options for higher-paying employment.

b.) Pay Off Debt: Set aside extra money to pay off debt in order to lower your overall monthly debt payments. To effectively pay off your obligations, take into account using debt repayment schemes like the debt snowball or debt avalanche approaches.

c.) Prevent Taking on New Debt: If you take on new debt, your DTI ratio may be negatively impacted. Before making large expenditures, explore other options or saving money first. Determine whether taking on new debt is necessary.

d.) Budgeting and Expense Management: Examine your spending plan and pinpoint places where you may reduce costs. Reduce your monthly debt payments by putting the funds towards debt repayment.

e.) Seek Professional Advice: If you're having trouble controlling your debt or lowering your DTI ratio, you might want to think about getting help from a financial advisor or credit counseling service. To assist you in overcoming your financial obstacles, they can offer you individualized counsel and direction.

Finally, the Debt-to-Income Ratio (DTI) is a crucial financial indicator that measures how well you are able to manage your debt in relation to your income. For budgeting success, financial stability, and loan eligibility, it's essential to monitor and maintain a healthy DTI ratio. You may make wise financial decisions and reach your long-term financial objectives by measuring your DTI ratio, analyzing the results, and taking proactive measures to improve it if necessary. Keep in mind that lowering your DTI ratio necessitates careful debt management, planning, and an emphasis on both raising your income and lowering your debt commitments.

Rule of 72

The Rule of 72 is a straightforward and practical formula for calculating how long it will take an investment, valued at an annual interest rate, to double in value. You may obtain an idea of how many years it would take for your money to double by dividing 72 by the yearly interest rate. Making wise financial decisions can be aided by using this guideline to gauge an investment's prospective growth. We will examine the Rule of 72 in depth in this section and offer real-world examples to demonstrate how it might be used.

1. **Recognising the Rule of 72:** Investors can use the Rule of 72 as a simple approximation to determine how long it will take for their assets to double. It is founded on the idea of compound interest, whereby interest from an investment is reinvested and, over time, experiences exponential growth.

The equation reads as follows:

72/ Annual interest rate

For instance, if your investment has an annual interest rate of 8%, you would divide 72 by 8 to get 9. This means that at an interest rate of 8%, it would take roughly 9 years for your money to double.

It's crucial to remember that the Rule of 72 just offers an approximation and takes the interest rate as constant. In actuality, inflation and other factors like fees and interest rates can have an impact on the growth of investments. The Rule of 72 is a useful tool for estimating the potential growth of an investment over time, though.

2. **Real-world Illustrations**: To further comprehend how the Rule of 72 is used in actual situations, let's look at some examples.

   Fixed Deposit Account, as an example.

Imagine you have a fixed deposit account earning 6% per year in interest. You can calculate how many years it would take for your investment to double by applying the Rule of 72:

12 years are required to double 72 years, or 6 years.

The time it would take for your investment in the fixed deposit account in this example to double at a 6% interest rate is roughly 12 years.

Example 2: ***Investing in the stock market***

Consider the possibility that you are thinking about buying a stock with a 10% average annual return in the past. You can evaluate the prospective development of your investment using the Rule of 72:

Years needed to double are equal to 72/10, or 7.2 years.

If the stock market had an average yearly return of 10%, it would take around 7.2 years for your investment to double.

Example 3: ***Investing in real estate***

Let's say you're thinking about buying a rental home that consistently earns 5% in annual returns. You can calculate how long it will take for your investment to double by using the Rule of 72:

72/5 = 14.4 years to twice the amount of time.

Therefore, assuming a 5% annual return, it would take roughly 14.4 years for your real estate investment to double.

The Rule of 72 can be used to calculate the doubling time for investments across a variety of asset types, as shown by the examples given above. The actual performance of investments, however, can vary, therefore it's important to keep in mind that additional aspects, such market conditions and personal circumstances, should also be considered.

3. **Limitations and Considerations:** The Rule of 72 is a helpful estimation tool, but it has several drawbacks that should be taken into account when assessing investments. Here are a few crucial things to remember:

The Rule of 72 presupposes a constant interest rate, which may not be practical in practice. a) Interest Rate Variability. Over time, interest rates may change, which could affect the growth of investments.

a.) **The Rule of Compounding Frequency:** 72 assumes annual compounding of interest. Compounding may actually happen more regularly, such as quarterly or monthly, which may have an impact on how long it actually takes for an investment to double.

b.) **Risk and Volatility:** The Rule of 72 ignores the risks and volatility connected to various investments. bigger-risk investments may have bigger potential returns, but they also carry more risk and a greater chance for loss.

c.) **Inflation:** The Rule of 72 does not take inflation's effect on investment returns into account. Over time, inflation devalues money's purchasing power, lowering the real rate of return on investments.

d.) **Diversification:** The Rule of 72 focuses on individual assets, but in order to manage risk and maximize long-term returns, it is crucial to take diversification across several asset classes into account.

4. **Applying the Rule of 72 Wisely:** The Rule of 72 can be used as a tool to determine when an investment will double in value, but it should also be utilized in conjunction with other financial factors. Here are some pointers for effectively applying the Rule of 72:

a.) **Recognise its Approximate Nature:** The Rule of 72 is an approximation and does not take into account all of the variables that can affect the growth of investments.

Use it as a starting point, but for a more precise assessment of an investment's possibilities, perform extensive research and analysis.

b.) **Take into Account Several Scenarios:** To comprehend the spectrum of possible outcomes, evaluate investments under various interest rate scenarios. You can assess the risk-return trade-off and make more educated decisions as a result.

c.) **Seek Professional Advice:** Consult a financial counselor if you have questions about applying the Rule of 72 or assessing investment opportunities. Based on your particular financial objectives, level of risk tolerance, and time horizon, they can offer tailored advice.

d.) **Conduct Regular Reviews and Adjustments:** Both investment environments and individual circumstances can alter over time. Review your investments frequently, and make necessary adjustments to your strategy to keep up with changing market conditions and your evolving goals.

The Rule of 72 is a useful calculator for determining how long it will take an investment to double based on the annual interest rate. Although it offers a rapid approximation, it's crucial to keep in mind its limitations and take other aspects into account when analyzing assets. You can make knowledgeable investing selections and work towards reaching your financial objectives by comprehending the Rule of 72, completing in-depth research, and consulting professionals if necessary.

Saving Rule:

Let's examine the savings rate concept in greater detail and use real-world examples to highlight its importance and potential applications in personal finance.

Knowing your savings rate is important since it indicates how much of your money you set aside each month for savings. It stands for the portion of your income that you set aside for present and future objectives, unexpected expenses, and investments. You can receive insight into your spending and saving priorities, measure your progress towards financial goals, and gain insight into your financial habits by calculating and tracking your savings rate.

The following equation can be used to get the savings rate:

(Monthly Savings Amount / Monthly Income) times 100 equals the savings rate.

Your savings rate, for instance, would be: if your monthly salary is Rs. 3,000 and you save Rs. 500 per month.

Rate of Savings = (500/3,000) x 100 = 16.67%

You are thus saving roughly 16.67% of your monthly salary.

The savings rate is an important indicator since it shows how well you are doing at building wealth and maintaining financial security. The savings rate is crucial for the following principal justifications:

a.) Saving a portion of your salary enables you to create an emergency fund, which serves as a safety net for your finances. You can avoid going into debt by using the money from an emergency fund to pay for unforeseen costs like medical bills, auto repairs, or job loss.

b.) Achieving Financial Goals: You can move closer to your financial objectives by continually saving more money and raising your savings rate. A greater savings rate makes it easier for you to reach your goals, whether they are saving for a down payment on a home, paying for your child's school, or making retirement plans.

c.) Building a Safety Net for Financial Independence: You can achieve financial independence by setting aside a sizable amount of your salary. Your ability to make decisions that are in line with your values and priorities, including pursuing a job change, establishing a business, or taking sabbaticals, is increased when your savings rate is higher.

d.) Creating Wealth Over Time: The savings rate is important for building wealth. You can benefit from compounding returns and increase your wealth over time by consistently saving and investing a bigger percentage of your income.

Practical Illustrations

To demonstrate the significance and practical use of the savings rate in real-life circumstances, let's look at a few concrete examples:

Example 1: The Influence of Regular Savings

A fresh college graduate named Sara begins her first job with a Rs. 2,500 monthly salary. She makes the decision to set aside 20% of her monthly income in order to create an emergency fund and save for the future. Following are the long-term effects of her savings rate on her financial situation:

Year 1: Savings each month equal 20% of Rs. 2,500, or Rs. 500.

Monthly Savings = Rs. 500 x 12 = Rs. 6,000

Year 5: Savings each month equal 20% of Rs. 2,500, or Rs. 500.

Monthly Savings = Rs. 500 x 12 = Rs. 6,000

Savings (Years 1-5): Rs. 6,000 multiplied by 5 is Rs. 30,000.

Year 10: Savings each month equal 20% of Rs. 2,500, or Rs. 500.

Monthly Savings = Rs. 500 x 12 = Rs. 6,000

Savings (Years 1-10): Rs. 6,000 multiplied by 10 is Rs. 60,000.

This illustration shows how regular higher-rate savings can result in significant savings over time. Over a ten-year period, Sara saves Rs. 60,000 by keeping her savings rate at 20%, giving her a strong financial foundation.

Example 2: Juggling expenses and savings

John, a working professional, makes Rs. 4,000 every month. He seeks to achieve a balance between living in the moment and saving for the future. He analyzes his spending and concludes that a savings rate of 30% is doable for him. His savings rate has the following effects on his financial situation:

Rs. 4000 monthly income

Savings per month: 30% of Rs. 4,000 equals Rs. 1,200

Expenses minus remaining income: Rs. 4,000 - Rs. 1,200 = Rs. 2,800

John prioritizes his long-term financial goals by setting aside Rs. 1,200 each month, which leaves him with Rs. 2,800 to cover his monthly needs such rent, utilities, groceries, and discretionary spending. As a result, he can continue to approach his financial security in a balanced manner.

Strategies to Boost Your Savings Rate: If you want to increase your savings rate, take into account the following tactics:

a.) **Monitor and Review Your Expenses:** Review your spending habits to locate areas where you may cut back on wasteful spending or seek out more economical options. This makes more money available for savings.

Set up automatic transfers from your checking account to a selected savings or investment account.

b.) Automate Your Savings: This guarantees ongoing savings without relying solely on willpower.

c.) Decrease Debt and Interest Payments: Eliminating high-interest debt, such credit card debt or personal loans, will considerably boost your savings rate.

Increased debt payback spending frees up future income for savings.

d.) Increase Your Income: Look into ways to increase your income, such as requesting a raise, accepting side jobs or freelance work, or investing in your education and professional development. More money can be saved as one makes more money.

e.) Set Realistic Goals: Establish clear, attainable financial objectives that encourage you to put money aside. Having specific goals will help you remain dedicated to raising your savings rate, whether they be for retirement, a trip, or a down payment.

f.) Continuously Monitor and Modify: Regularly assess your spending patterns, savings rate, and financial objectives. If your income or circumstances change, you should update your savings rate to reflect the new state of your finances.

You may steadily raise your savings rate and go a lot closer to accomplishing your financial objectives by putting these ideas into practice and keeping dedicated to saving.

In conclusion, the savings rate, which calculates the percentage of your income that you set aside each month, is a key idea in personal finance. You can establish an emergency fund, strive towards financial objectives, and lay a strong basis for long-term financial well-being by being aware of and actively controlling your savings rate. You may achieve your financial goals by taking actionable steps like consistently conserving money and keeping costs in check. Keep in mind that growing your savings rate is a process that calls for self-control, thoughtfulness, and routine examination of your spending patterns and financial objectives.

Compound Interest:

Four main elements make up compound interest:

Principal (P): Your initial investment or loan will include a principal component. It is the basis for computing compound interest. The principle in our previous illustration was Rs. 1,000.

Annual interest rate (r): The annual interest rate (r) is a measure of how much interest will be accrued or imposed annually on the principal sum. The interest rate in our scenario was 5%.

Annual number of compounding periods (n): Compounding might take place every day, every six months, every three months, or even every year. The number of times the interest is compounded and applied to the principle depends on the compounding period. Since compounding happened yearly in our scenario, n was equal to 1.

The number of years for which the money is invested or lent is represented by the time (t). The investment in our example was kept for three years.

Let's now examine the compound interest formula and its application in real life:

A = P(1 + r/n)nt

After compound interest is taken into account, the formula determines the final sum (A).

Let's think about a situation where you put Rs. 1,000 into an account for three years at 5% per year with annual compounding (n = 1).

Year 1: The interest earned is calculated as P * (r/n) at the conclusion of the first year, which in our example is Rs. 1,000 * (0.05/1) = Rs. 50. The principal is increased by this interest, creating a new principal for the following year.

Year 2: The interest is computed based on the new principal of Rs. 1,050 in the second year. Therefore, Rs. 1,050 * (0.05/1) = Rs. 52.50 is the interest earned in the second year. Once more, the principal is increased by this interest.

Year 3: The interest is computed based on the new principal of Rs. 1,102.50 in the third year. Rs. 1,102.50 * (0.05/1) = Rs. 55.13 represents the interest earned.

The total amount (A) at the end of the third year equals the sum of the principal plus accrued interest, or Rs. 1,157.63 (Rs. 1,102.50 + Rs. 55.13).

As you can see, compound interest enables the exponential growth of your investment over time. Each period's interest is added to the principal, and subsequent interest calculations are made using the bigger, newly created principal. When compared to simple interest, this compounding effect results in a bigger total sum.

Savings accounts, fixed deposits, bonds, and loans are just a few examples of financial instruments that frequently use compound interest. When assessing the prospective growth or cost of an investment or loan, it's crucial to take the frequency of compounding, interest rate, and time period into account.

Individuals who comprehend compound interest are better equipped to achieve their long-term financial objectives and make wise financial judgements.

Debt Payoff Strategy:

People and families who are in debt may find it difficult to maintain their financial security and pursue their future ambitions. People frequently use debt payback solutions to overcome their debt and restore control over their finances. The Avalanche Method and the Snowball Method are two widely utilized methods, including in India. In this thorough presentation, we will examine these tactics in the context of India and provide real-world examples to show how powerful they are.

Snowball Method: Regardless of the interest rates attached to each obligation, the Snowball Method focuses on paying off debts from the smallest balance to the greatest balance. This strategy's main goal is to build momentum and drive by completing little victories and paying off lesser obligations.

Let's dissect the Snowball Method in detail:

List your debts first:

Make a thorough record of every debt you have, including

credit card debt, personal loans, auto loans, student loans, and any other outstanding sums. Make care to record each debt's current balance, required minimum payment, and interest rate.

Let's take the following debts, for instance:

Debt 1: Credit Card A with a balance of Rs. 50,000, a Rs. 5,000 minimum payment, and an interest rate of 18%

Debt 2: Personal Loan B, with a debt of Rs. 2,00,000 and a minimum payment of Rs. 10,000 at a 12% interest rate.

Debt 3: Car Loan C with a debt of Rs. 8,00,000 and a minimum payment of Rs. 20,000 at a 10% interest rate

Step 2: Pay the Minimums. To avoid fees and keep your credit score high, make sure you pay each debt the minimum amount due on time. It's important to set aside enough money in your budget for these minimal payments.

Step 3: Distribute additional funds:

Calculate how much additional cash you can set aside each month to pay off debt. Look for places where you may cut costs or think about boosting your sources of revenue. The more you can set aside, the quicker you'll be able to pay off your debt.

Step 4: Pay down the smallest debt initially:

Apply the extra money you set aside to the debt with the lowest balance while still making the minimum payments on the other obligations. The quickest debt repayment is the objective.

Assume you have an extra Rs. 10,000 each month to go towards paying off debt. You would apply the remaining Rs. 5,000 towards this debt after paying the Rs. 5,000 minimum payment on Credit Card A. You will have fully paid off Credit Card A in ten months.

Step 5: Transfer payments to the following debt

Apply the total amount you were paying towards the smallest obligation (minimum payment plus additional cash) to the next loan on your list once the smallest debt has been paid off. In our scenario, you will devote Rs. 15,000 (Rs. 5,000 minimum payment + Rs. 10,000 excess money) to Personal Loan B after paying off Credit Card A.

With the same Rs. 15,000 monthly payment schedule, it will take roughly 16 months to pay off Personal Loan B in full.

Step 6: Repeat and expedite: Continue making payments towards one obligation after another until all outstanding balances have been paid off. As you observe debts being paid off one at a time using this strategy, you gain momentum and motivation.

In our scenario, you will devote Rs. 35,000 (Rs. 15,000 minimum payment + Rs. 20,000 excess money) towards Car Loan C after paying off Personal Loan B. It will take about 23 months to finish off Car Loan C with this accelerated payback.

You may successfully prioritize and pay off your obligations by using the Snowball Method, which will give you a sense of accomplishment and enable you to become debt-free in the long run.

Another well-liked debt repayment method is the avalanche

method, which emphasizes paying off the loans with the highest interest rates first. Because it reduces the total interest paid during the payback period, this approach is profitable.

Let's look more closely at the Avalanche Method:

List your debts first:

Make a note of every debt you have, including credit card balances, personal loans, auto loans, student loans, and any other outstanding liabilities. Make a note of each debt's current balance, required minimum payment, and interest rate.

Let's take the following debts, for instance:

Debt 1: Credit Card A with a balance of Rs. 50,000, a Rs. 5,000 minimum payment, and an interest rate of 18%

Debt 2: Personal Loan B, with a debt of Rs. 2,00,000 and a minimum payment of Rs. 10,000 at a 12% interest rate.

Debt 3: Car Loan C with a debt of Rs. 8,00,000 and a minimum payment of Rs. 20,000 at a 10% interest rate

Step 2: Pay the minimums. To avoid fees and keep your credit score high, make sure to pay each debt's minimum payment due on time. Make sure your budget includes enough money to make these minimal payments.

Step 3: Distribute additional funds:

Calculate how much additional cash you can set aside each month to pay off debt. Review your spending plan, look for places where you may cut costs, and look for ways to boost your revenue.

The Avalanche Method, in contrast to the Snowball Method, prioritizes paying off debts with the highest interest rates first. Step 4: Pay off highest interest debt. Apply the additional money you set aside to the debt with the highest interest rate while paying the minimum amount towards the other bills.

The Credit Card A in our illustration has the highest interest rate at 18%. After paying the minimal amount of Rs. 5,000 for Credit Card A, you would then apply the remaining Rs. 5,000 towards this obligation, assuming you have an additional Rs. 10,000 per month to devote to debt reduction. Approximately 11 months will pass before Credit Card A is paid off.

Step 5: Transfer payments to the following debt

Apply the total amount you were paying towards it (minimum payment plus additional cash) to the next loan on your list once the debt with the highest interest rate has been settled. In our scenario, you will devote Rs. 15,000 (Rs. 5,000 minimum payment + Rs. 10,000 excess money) to Personal Loan B after paying off Credit Card A.

With the same Rs. 15,000 monthly payment schedule, it will take roughly 19 months to pay off Personal Loan B in full.

Step 6: Repetition and quickening

Roll over the payments to the following debt on the list as each debt is paid off to ensure that all debts are paid off. This strategy speeds up debt repayment while lowering the overall amount of interest paid.

You will set aside Rs. 35,000 (Rs. 15,000 minimum payment + Rs. 20,000 excess cash) for Car Loan C after paying off Personal Loan B. It will take about 23 months to finish off Car Loan C with this accelerated payback.

You may prioritize high-interest loans and make progress towards debt freedom more quickly by using the Avalanche Method.

Considerations and Comparison:

The Snowball Method is advantageous for people who value the psychological impact of early victories and momentum. You will feel more accomplished and motivated if you pay off minor obligations first. However, if higher-interest obligations are not prioritized, using this strategy can lead to paying more interest over time.

Avalanche Method: Because it reduces the overall interest paid over the payback period, the Avalanche Method is advantageous from a financial standpoint. Long-term financial savings are possible if you concentrate on high-interest bills. However, because higher-interest debts typically have higher balances, using this strategy can take longer to provide noticeable gains.

Selecting the Best Approach for You:

Choose between the Snowball Method and the Avalanche Method after taking your financial objectives, preferences, and the specifics of your obligations into account. Determine which will help your priorities more: the psychological high of small victories (Snowball Method) or the monetary gain of interest savings (Avalanche Method).

It's crucial to remember that there are other debt repayment methods besides the Snowball and Avalanche Methods. Other tactics, such debt negotiation or consolidation, might also be worthwhile to investigate. The secret is to approach debt repayment proactively and develop a plan that works for your particular situation.

Dealing with debt might be overwhelming, but with the appropriate plan and perseverance, you can take back control of your finances. In the Indian setting, the Snowball Method and the Avalanche Method offer efficient frameworks for debt repayment. You can successfully pay off your debts and gain financial freedom by adhering to these tactics and consistently making an effort to set aside additional money for debt reduction. Remember to take into account your particular circumstance and select the strategy that best suits your objectives and preferences.

Net Worth Calculation:

Calculating Your Net Worth: Assessing Your Financial Situation

A financial indicator called net worth gives you a general picture of your financial situation. It stands for the distinction between your liabilities (what you owe) and your assets (what you own). You can acquire important insights into your financial development and make wise choices regarding wealth-building tactics by routinely measuring and tracking your net worth. This in-depth explanation will examine the idea of net worth, highlight its importance, and offer real-world examples to make it easier for you to comprehend and determine your own net worth.

Assets are the valuable possessions you own. They can be divided into several categories, such as:

a.) **Cash and Cash Equivalents:** The funds in your bank accounts, cash on hand, and any other liquid assets that are easily convertible into cash fall under this category.

b.) **Investments:** This area includes any other investments you may have made, as well as stocks, bonds, mutual funds, real estate, and retirement accounts.

c.) **Physical Assets:** These are things you own that have a physical form and have worth, such as your house, car, jewelry, works of art, furniture, and other personal belongings.

d.) **Other Assets:** Any additional assets you may have, such as business ownership, patents, copyrights, or other valuable intellectual property, fall under this category.

You must ascertain the overall value of your assets by adding the values of each category in order to establish your net worth.

Let's take the following assets, for instance:

2,00,000 in cash and cash equivalents.

Amount Invested: Rs. 8,000,000.

Physical assets include a home worth Rs. 50,000 and vehicles worth Rs. 20,000.

Other Resources: Ownership of a business: Rs. 15,000

Total Assets = Rs. 2.00 + Rs. 8.00 + Rs. 50.00 + Rs. 10.00 + Rs. 15.00 = Rs. 85.00

The entire asset value in this instance is Rs. 85,000,000.

Liabilities: Liabilities are the commitments or debts you owe to other people.

They may consist of:

a.) **A mortgage,** which is the remaining debt on any loans secured by real estate, including your home loan.

b.) **Personal Loans:** These are loans you have taken out for other non-business reasons, such education, travel, or debt relief.

c.) **Credit Card Debt:** This refers to any outstanding charges on your credit cards.

d.) **Auto Loans:** These are loans you take out to pay for your cars.

e.) **Other Debts:** Included in this category are any other unpaid debts, including credit card balances, business loans, and medical bills.

You must tally up the outstanding amounts of each category to get the total value of your liabilities in order to calculate your net worth.

Let's take the following obligations, for instance:

Mortgage: 40,000 rupees

Personal loans: 5,000 rupees

Debt on Credit Cards: Rs. 100,000

6,00,000 in auto loans

2,00,000 in other debt

Total Liabilities equal Rs. 40,00,000 plus Rs. 5,00,000 plus Rs. 1,00,000 plus Rs. 6,00,000 plus Rs. 2,000,000.

Liabilities in this illustration total Rs. 54,000,000.

Calculating Net Worth: Once the total value of your assets and obligations has been established, you can calculate your net worth by deducting the value of your liabilities from the value of your assets.

Total Assets - Total Liabilities equals Net Worth.

Using the preceding examples:

Net Worth is equal to Rs. 54,00,000 less Rs. 85,00,000, or Rs. 31,00,000.

The calculated net value in this case is Rs. 31,000,000.

Meaning of Net Worth: Net worth is an important financial indicator for numerous reasons, including:

a.) **Evaluation of Financial Health:** By taking into account both your assets and obligations, net worth offers a complete picture of your financial health. It gives you a picture of your total financial situation and can reveal whether you are increasing your wealth or taking on additional debt.

b.) **Progress Monitoring:** By routinely assessing your net worth, you may monitor your financial development over time. You may evaluate the effects of your financial actions and modify your tactics by keeping an eye on changes in your net worth.

c.) **Goal Setting and Planning:** Having an understanding of your net worth can help you create money-related objectives and design sensible wealth-building strategies. It gives you a sense of where you are right now and serves as a starting point for planning the activities necessary to reach your targeted financial goals.

d.) **Financial Decision-Making:** Your net worth may have an impact on your financial decision-making. Knowing your net worth, for instance, might help you assess the potential effects on your total financial situation whether you're thinking about making a significant purchase, taking advantage of an investment opportunity, or taking on more debt.

Let's look at a few real-world instances to illustrate the importance of calculating net worth:

Example 1: Mr. Sharma's total assets, which include his house, his investments, and his cash equivalents, total Rs. 1,600,000. He also has liabilities, such as his credit card and mortgage loan, totaling Rs. 1,20,000,000. To determine his net worth:

Net worth is equal to Rs. 1,50,000,000 minus Rs. 1,20,000, or Rs. 30,00,000.

The total wealth of Mr. Sharma is Rs. 30,000,000. According to this data, he has amassed a sizable amount of wealth in comparison to his liabilities.

Example 2: Ms. Verma has financial interests and material possessions totaling Rs. 50,000,000. However, her liabilities, which include her mortgage, auto loan, and personal debts, amount Rs. 60,000,000. To determine her net worth:

Net worth is equal to Rs. 50,000, minus Rs. 60,000, or Rs. 10,000.

The amount of Ms. Verma's net worth is Rs. 100,000. Due to her negative net worth, it appears that she has more liabilities than assets, necessitating debt management and wealth-building techniques.

In conclusion, calculating your net worth is a crucial step in evaluating your financial situation, monitoring your development, and making wise choices. You can obtain important insights into your financial situation, spot opportunities for improvement, and start the process of accumulating wealth by routinely assessing your net worth using an understanding of your assets, liabilities, and other financial commitments. To lay a strong basis for your financial future, think about including net worth calculation in your entire financial management. Review and update your net worth frequently to track your progress and make any required modifications to your financial plans.

Keep in mind that net worth is not a constant figure and can change over time. It is impacted by a number of variables, including modifications to your liabilities, interest rate swings, and alterations to the value of your assets. You may better understand your financial condition and make wise decisions to enhance your overall financial well-being by continuously keeping track of your net worth.

Finally, your net worth is a crucial indicator of your financial well-being. By taking into account your assets and liabilities, it gives you a quick overview of your financial situation. You may assess your progress, establish financial objectives, and take well-informed decisions to better your financial status by periodically measuring and monitoring your net worth. To calculate your net worth, start by making a list of your assets and obligations, adding up the totals, and then deducting your liabilities from your assets. Build a strong foundation for a safe and prosperous future using the advice in this article to help you with your financial planning.

Saving for Retirement: Creating a Secure Future

To ensure financial independence and stability in your later years, you must save for retirement. It is commonly advised to set aside 10–15 percent of your salary for retirement. This includes making contributions to 401(k) and IRA retirement accounts. Your ability to expand your retirement savings can be significantly impacted by starting early and taking advantage of company matching programmes. We will go through the significance of saving for retirement, the general saving rule, real-world examples, and techniques to make the most of your retirement assets in this thorough discussion.

Savings for retirement are essential for a number of reasons, including:

a.) **Financial independence:** By setting aside money for retirement, you are creating a fund that will keep you afloat once you stop working. During your retirement years, it enables you to maintain your standard of living and pay for bills.

b.) **Compound Interest:** By routinely setting aside money early on, you can take advantage of compounding. Your contributions generate returns over time, and those returns generate returns as well, causing your retirement savings to increase more quickly.

c.) **Inflation Protection:** Retirement savings assist mitigate the effects of inflation. Having a sizable retirement fund means that you can afford the costs related to retirement as the cost of living rises over time.

Adequate retirement savings give you flexibility and peace of mind, allowing you to follow your interests, travel, or spend time with family without worrying about running out of money.

The general rule of thumb for retirement savings is setting aside between 10% and 15% of your salary. Your contributions and any employer matching contributions are both included in this proportion. The precise amount you should save, however, will depend on a number of variables, including your age, salary, anticipated retirement lifestyle, and other financial commitments.

The general rule of thumb advises saving between Rs. 1,000,000 and Rs. 1,5,000,000 each year for retirement, for instance, if your annual income is Rs. 10,000,000.

The rule of thumb should be understood as a general guideline, and people with particular circumstances may need to modify their savings rate. A financial advisor you consult with can offer you individualized guidance based on your particular circumstances.

Examples of Realistic Retirement Savings:

To further understand the impact of retirement savings, let's look at a few real-world examples:

Example 1: Sarah, who is 30 years old, has a yearly salary of Rs. 6,00,000. She makes the decision to save 10% of her income each year for retirement. This indicates that she will put aside Rs. 60,000 annually for her retirement.

Her retirement funds might increase dramatically over time if she keeps saving Rs. 60,000 a year until she turns 65 and assumes an average annual return of 7%.

We may calculate Sarah's prospective retirement savings using a retirement calculator:

Contributions in total: Rs. 60,000 annually for 35 years, or

Rs. 21,00,000.

Value Projected at Retirement: Rs. 21,00,000 + Investment Returns

If returns were to average 7%, Sarah's retirement fund might increase to about Rs. 1,34,60,000.

Example 2: John, who is 45 years old, earns Rs. 15,00,000 per year. He makes the decision to save 15% of his income each year for retirement. This implies that he will put up Rs. 2,25,000 annually for his retirement.

His retirement funds would increase over time if he keeps saving Rs. 2,25,000 per year until he is 65 and assumes an average yearly return of 7%.

We may calculate John's prospective retirement savings using a retirement calculator:

Total Contributions: 2,25,000 rupees a year multiplied by 20 years equals 45,00,000.

Retirement Estimated Value: Rs. 50,000, plus Investment Returns

If returns were to average 7%, John's retirement funds might increase to about Rs. 1,22,000,000.

Tips for Increasing Retirement Savings:

If you want to increase your retirement funds, think about the following tactics:

a.) **Begin Early:** Because of the power of compounding, beginning early is essential. Your money has more time to grow the longer it is invested. Even modest contributions made often over an extended period of time can produce sizable retirement savings.

b.) **Benefit from Employer Matching:** If your employer provides a retirement plan with a matching contribution, make at least the minimum contribution to qualify for the maximum match. Employer matching can greatly increase your retirement savings because they are practically free money.

c.) **Increase Contributions Over Time:** Take into account raising your retirement contributions as your income rises or your expenses fall. To make sure you are on pace to attain your retirement objectives, aim to gradually reach or surpass the suggested savings rate.

d.) **Diversify Your Investments:** To diversify your portfolio, spread out your retirement assets among various asset types. In the long run, this increases the possibility of better returns while assisting in risk management.

e.) **Regularly Review and Adjust:** Track the development of your retirement savings on a regular basis. If circumstances or market conditions change, you may need to adjust your retirement goals, investment allocations, and contributions.

Saving for retirement is essential for ensuring a future of financial independence. A basic guideline is to save 10-15% of your income, including employer matching contributions, for retirement. The appropriate savings rate, however, may change depending on a person's unique situation. Your retirement savings may be greatly impacted by starting early and utilizing company matches. You can work towards constructing a solid nest egg that supports your desired retirement lifestyle by paying attention to realistic instances and putting techniques to maximize your retirement finances into practice. Always keep an eye on your savings, make any modifications, and seek personalized advice from a financial counselor.

Housing Affordability:

The ability of individuals or households to easily pay for housing expenses without jeopardizing their overall financial stability is a critical component of personal finance. When choosing between renting and buying a property, as well as when planning your budget for housing-related costs, it is an essential factor to take into account. A frequently accepted rule of thumb recommends that people should spend no more than 30% of their monthly income on housing costs, which includes rent or mortgage payments, property taxes, and insurance. To maintain sustainable housing costs in the Indian context, it is crucial to go deeper into the idea of housing affordability, examine the elements that affect it, and take into account real-world examples and initiatives.

1. **Understanding Housing Affordability:** The ability of people or households to easily fulfill their housing bills while maintaining a stable financial existence is referred

to as housing affordability. It considers a number of things, including personal circumstances, housing costs, other financial responsibilities, and income. Striking a balance between housing costs and other fundamental necessities, savings, and long-term financial objectives is the main objective.

2. **The 30% Rule of Thumb:** This is a general principle for determining the affordability of housing. It recommends that people or households spend no more than 30% of their monthly income on housing. This regulation was created by the U.S. Department of Housing and Urban Development (HUD) and has spread to several nations, including India, where it is now used as a standard for housing affordability.

The 30% rule, for instance, states that if a person makes Rs. 50,000 a month, their total housing costs, including rent or mortgage payments, property taxes, and insurance, shouldn't be more than Rs. 15,000 (30% of Rs. 50,000).

2. **Real-world illustrations of housing affordability:** Let's look at a few real-world examples to help us better comprehend the concept of affordable housing:

Example 1: Renting a Property Let's say someone makes Rs. 60,000 a month. The 30% rule states that in order to ensure affordability, their housing costs should not be higher than Rs. 18,000 (30% of Rs. 60,000).

If they can locate a rental home for Rs. 15,000 a month, their housing expenditures will fall inside the suggested limit. However, the 30% threshold would be exceeded if they came upon a rental property that cost Rs. 25,000 per month. To secure affordable accommodation in this situation, they might need to look into other possibilities, haggle over the rent, or change their spending plan.

Mortgage payments, as an example.

Let's say a household makes Rs. 1,20,000 per month in total. To ensure affordability, they should adhere to the 30% rule, which states that their monthly housing costs, including mortgage payments, should not be higher than Rs. 36,000 (30% of Rs.

They determine that they can afford a monthly mortgage payment of about Rs 30,000 by taking into account the loan terms, current interest rates, and their financial situation. This is within the advised affordability range, enabling them to afford their mortgage while comfortably managing their finances.

When assessing the affordability of homeownership, it is crucial to take additional housing expenses like property taxes, insurance, and upkeep into account. To ensure a thorough evaluation of housing affordability, these costs should also be taken into account when calculating the 30% guideline.

3. **Personal Factors Affecting Housing Affordability:**

The 30% rule of thumb is a good place to start, but it's also important to take into account each person's unique position and assess housing affordability in the context of their own financial circumstances. Here are some important things to think about:

a.) **Debt Obligations:** People or households with a

lot of debt, including credit card debt or school loans, may need to change their housing budget. To maintain a good balance between debt management and home affordability, allocating a higher percentage of income towards debt repayment may need restricting housing costs.

b.) **Savings Objectives:** It's crucial to set aside money for savings objectives while taking house affordability into account. Whether the objective is to gather cash for a down payment on a home, save for retirement, or develop an emergency fund, people should adjust their housing budget to accommodate these savings contributions.

c.) **Cost of Living:** In India, the cost of living differs between various states, towns, and localities. To make sure that the housing budget is in line with the current market conditions, housing affordability should be assessed in the context of the local cost of living. For instance, compared to smaller towns, housing expenses may be greater in large cities like Mumbai or Delhi.

d.) **Lifestyle Factors:** Personal preferences and lifestyle dccisions can affect a person's capacity to finance a home. Housing expenses may be influenced by elements including desired neighborhood, facilities, and living standards. It is crucial to evaluate these elements and make informed judgements that are in line with one's priorities and resources.

e.) **Financial Goals and Risk Tolerance:** Every person has different financial goals and levels of risk tolerance. If it fits with their priorities and financial goals, some people might feel at ease putting a larger portion of their income towards housing costs. Assessing long-term financial objectives and risk tolerance is critical when figuring out whether a home is affordable.

6. **Housing Cost Management Techniques:** People should think about the following tactics to maintain sustainable housing costs:

   a.) **Budgeting:** Create a thorough budget that accounts for all sources of income, expenses, and financial objectives. Set aside money for other necessary requirements and savings while giving housing costs the highest priority within the 30% limit.

   b.) **Down Payment and Loan Terms:** When buying a home, setting aside money for a sizable down payment can assist lower the loan amount and related mortgage payments. Investigating various loan terms and interest rates can also maximize affordability. A financial counselor or mortgage broker can be a great source of information.

   c.) **Rent Negotiation:** When renting a property, bargain for a rent that is within your means. Particularly in places with high vacancy rates or during economic downturns, landlords might be amenable to conversations.

   d.) **Affordable Housing Options:** Look into affordable housing programmes offered by the government or nonprofit organizations, co-living spaces, or shared accommodations. These choices can lower home costs while preserving convenience and comfort.

e.) **Periodic Financial Review:** Examine your financial situation and reevaluate your ability to afford a home. The housing budget may need to be modified due to changes in income, expenses, or personal circumstances. A balanced financial life can be maintained by taking the initiative and making the required adjustments.

f.) **Seek Professional Advice:** A financial planner or advisor can offer tailored advice based on specific circumstances. They can assist in analyzing financial problems, determining the affordability of home, and creating a thorough strategy that is in line with certain goals and objectives.

Housing affordability is a crucial component of personal finance since it has a direct impact on a person's or family's capacity to maintain their financial stability and general well-being. A general formula for allocating income towards housing costs is the 30% rule of thumb. When assessing housing affordability, it's crucial to take into account personal factors like debt responsibilities, savings objectives, cost of living, lifestyle preferences, and risk tolerance. People can make sure that their housing costs stay within a tolerable range by applying realistic examples, taking into account personal considerations, and putting sustainable ideas into practice. A healthy financial life will result from routinely evaluating and modifying home costs as necessary. A financial advisor can offer personalized advice and improve decision-making in terms of property affordability.

Formula for Repaying Student Loans: Debt-to-Income Ratio (DTI)

For people in India, the debt-to-income ratio (DTI) is a helpful financial tool for calculating a realistic student loan repayment amount. It gauges how much of your gross monthly income goes towards paying down debt each month. You may determine your capacity to manage additional debt and make well-informed decisions about your student loan repayment strategy by understanding and calculating your DTI. To prevent having too much debt, it is advised to aim for a DTI ratio of less than 15%.

Follow these procedures to determine your DTI in the Indian context:

Calculate the total monthly debt payments in step one.

Calculate your total recurring loan payments first. This includes any unpaid credit card balances, personal loans, student loans, and other debts that you are accountable for.

Let's imagine, for illustration, that you must make the following monthly debt payments:

Paying off student loans: Rs. 10,000

Payment for a personal loan: Rs. 5,000

Payment using a credit card: Rs. 2,000

Total Monthly Debt Payments equal Rs. 10,000 + Rs. 5,000

+ Rs. 2,000 = Rs. 17,000

Calculate your gross monthly income in Step 2

Next, figure out your monthly gross revenue. The whole amount of your income before any withholdings or taxes is shown here. Include all income sources, including salary, bonuses, allowances, and any other regular income.

Let's imagine, for illustration, that your gross monthly revenue is Rs. 50,000.

Calculate the DTI Ratio in Step 3

To represent the ratio as a percentage, divide your total monthly debt payments by your gross monthly income and multiply the result by 100.

Total Monthly Debt Payments / Gross Monthly Income multiplied by 100 is the DTI Ratio.

Let's determine the DTI ratio utilizing the example values:

(Rs. 17,000 / Rs. 50,000) x 100 = 34% is the DTI Ratio.

The DTI ratio in this case is 34%, beyond the suggested range of 10-15%. In order to ensure a more manageable amount of debt, you may need to reassess your budget and repayment plan as a result of the fact that a sizable portion of your income is going into debt payments.

DTI Ratio Interpretation:

DTI Ratio less than 10%: This indicates a modest debt load compared to income, showing that you have the money to comfortably manage increased debt payments.

DTI Ratio of 10% to 15%: This range of debt is typically seen as manageable. It shows that you set aside a healthy amount of your salary for debt repayments, leaving money for savings and other financial commitments.

DTI Ratio more than 15%: This denotes a higher debt load in comparison to income. It shows that a sizable amount of your income is already going towards debt repayments, which might make it more difficult for you to take on new debt or save enough money.

In the Indian context, using the DTI ratio for student loan repayment:

When deciding on a comfortable amount for student loan repayment, you can use your DTI ratio as a guideline. You can determine whether or not your current student loan payments fall within a fair range based on your income and other financial commitments.

If your DTI ratio is higher than 15%, you might want to think about debt-reduction plans. This may entail looking into possibilities like refinancing your student loans to get better terms, modifying your repayment strategy to lengthen the repayment period and lower monthly payments, or finding ways to boost your income to better handle your debt responsibilities.

However, if your DTI ratio is between 10% and 15%, you will often be able to manage your student loan payments. However, it's still vital to carefully examine your spending plan, take into account your long-term financial objectives, and make sure that paying back your student loans fits into your overall financial strategy.

It's important to keep in mind that the DTI ratio is only one aspect to take into account when choosing your student loan repayment plan. It is important to consider additional elements as well, such as interest rates, loan periods, and prospective loan forgiveness programmes. A financial advisor or student loan specialist can offer insightful advice that is suited to your particular situation.

In conclusion, people in India can utilize the Debt-to-Income Ratio (DTI) to gauge their capacity to handle student loan repayment. You can calculate a realistic amount for student loan payments and make decisions about your overall financial health by calculating your DTI ratio and comparing it to the advised standards. For the purpose of creating a thorough plan for repaying student loans, it is crucial to take the DTI ratio into account with other variables and to obtain professional help when necessary.

Cost per Credit Hour Formula:

Students in India can assess the cost-effectiveness of various courses or academic programmes using the cost per credit hour calculation. It enables students to contrast the costs related to obtaining credit across multiple courses or organizations. Students can make educated decisions regarding their educational investments and select courses or programmes that are in line with their financial objectives by estimating the cost per credit hour. The number of credit hours taken is divided by the total cost of tuition for the semester or school year.

Let's break down the cost per credit hour formula into steps to make it easier to comprehend and use:

Step 1: Determine the total cost of tuition.

Determine the overall tuition expense for a certain time frame, such as a semester or academic year. Tuition, registration, and any other costs directly connected to the educational programme are included here. In order to get a clear image of the required financial commitment, it is crucial to take into account all pertinent charges.

Let's use the case of someone seeking a bachelor's degree in engineering, whose tuition will total Rs. 80,000 for one semester. This sum covers tuition, testing fees, and other associated costs.

Step 2: Calculate the Total Credit Hours

Next, figure out how many credits each of the courses you intend to take over the selected time period carries. The amount of effort or academic value attributed to each course is expressed in credit hours. They give an indication of the time and effort needed to finish the course. Credit hours often range from 1 to 4, depending on how intense and in-depth the subject is.

The overall number of credit hours for the semester would be 5 x 3 = 15 credit hours, for example, if you were enrolled in five courses for the semester, each worth three credits.

Step 3: Apply the Cost per Credit Hour formula.

By dividing the overall cost of tuition by the number of credit hours, you can now determine the price per credit hour using the information you have acquired.

Cost per Credit Hour is calculated as Total Tuition and Credits.

Using the values from the example:

Rs. 80,000 / 15 = Rs. 5,333.33 for the cost per credit hour.

As a result, the price per credit hour for the semester of your choice is Rs. 5,333.33.

How to Interpret the Price Per Credit Hour:

The price per credit hour gives information on how financially efficient various courses or academic programmes are. Students can examine the relative affordability of different disciplines or universities and the investment needed for each credit hour obtained thanks to this information.

Take into account the following details when assessing the cost per credit hour:

A more inexpensive course or programme will have a lower cost per credit hour. It implies that for every rupee paid, you are receiving higher intellectual value.

Value for Money: Along with the school's standing, faculty members' qualifications, and the resources provided to students, the cost per credit hour should be assessed. The whole educational experience and the chances for learning and growth must be balanced with cost effectiveness.

Return on Investment: Evaluate the prospective return on investment by taking into account the potential earnings and employment opportunities connected to the selected course or programme. If it results with greater future career chances and income, a higher cost per credit hour might be acceptable.

Scholarships & Financial Aid: Be aware that financial aid packages, grants, and scholarships can dramatically lower the cost per credit hour. Investigate your options for financial support and assess the effect on your overall spending.

Consider your long-term educational and professional ambitions when making future plans. While the price per credit hour is important, it should also be considered in light of your goals as well as the abilities and information you hope to gain.

You may make wise selections regarding your educational investments by calculating and comparing the price per credit hour for various courses or programmes. It enables you to evaluate the financial effects of every credit hour gained and select the solutions that are the most affordable. However, keep in mind that when choosing a course of study, there are many other factors to take into account. Along with other elements including curriculum, faculty, reputation, and individual goals, it should be assessed.

When using the cost per credit hour method, it's important to do extensive research, speak with academic counselors, and take your particular financial position and ambitions into account. Additionally, bear in mind that prices for education in India can differ between institutions, courses, and areas. As a result, it's crucial to have precise and current information from the particular educational institutions you're thinking about.

You can make educated choices about your educational experience in India by using the cost per credit hour method and taking the bigger picture into account.

Let's get into the formula for cost per credit hour in greater detail.

Step 1: Determine the total cost of tuition.

You must first estimate the overall cost of tuition for a certain time period, such as a semester or academic year, in order to compute the price per credit hour. This includes any additional fees or costs specifically associated with the educational programme in addition to the tuition fees levied by the educational institution. The following are some typical elements of the overall cost of tuition:

Tuition: The main expense related to enrolling in classes and attending an educational institution is tuition. Depending on the school, the course of study, and the level of education (undergraduate, postgraduate, etc.), tuition costs might vary significantly.

Registration Fees: At the start of each academic semester, many educational institutions charge a registration or enrollment fee. This money assists in reserving your spot in the programme and goes towards administrative expenses.

Exam fees: Some universities charge extra money for exams or evaluations that are given throughout the semester or at the conclusion of the course.

Fees for the use of specialized laboratories or equipment may be necessary for some courses or programmes, particularly those in the sciences, engineering, or healthcare sectors. Additional fees might be levied in certain circumstances to cover the costs of maintenance and usage.

Textbooks and Course Materials: The price of textbooks and other educational resources may increase the total cost of tuition. Depending on the programme and the particular courses attended, these costs may change.

For a precise estimate of the entire cost of tuition, it is crucial to take into account all the pertinent expenses related to the study term you have chosen.

Step 2: Calculate the Total Credit Hours

The next step is to figure out how many credits are required for the courses you want to take during the selected time frame. The amount of effort or academic value attributed to each course is expressed in credit hours. They give an indication of the time and effort needed to finish the course. Credit hours often range from 1 to 4, depending on how intense and in-depth the subject is.

Each course's credit hours are typically listed in the curriculum guide or course catalog that the educational institution provides. To get this information, you can also speak with department heads or academic advisors. Include any course you intend to take during the particular time frame being considered.

Step 3: Apply the Cost per Credit Hour formula.

You may calculate the price per credit hour by dividing the total cost of tuition by the number of credit hours once you know the total cost of tuition and the number of credits.

Cost per Credit Hour is calculated as Total Tuition and Credits.

Let's use the following case to demonstrate:

Consider that the whole cost of tuition for one semester for a Bachelor's degree in Commerce is Rs. 60,000.

For the semester, you want to enroll in five courses with the following credit hours:

Course 1: Four credits

Course 2: Three credits

Course 3: Three credits

Course 4: Two credits

Course 5: Two Credits

For the semester, there will be 14 credit hours overall (4 + 3 + 3 + 2 + 2).

Let's now determine the price per credit hour:

Price per credit hour is calculated as Rs. 60,000 / 14 = Rs. 4,285.71.

As a result, this semester's price per credit hour is roughly Rs. 4,285.71.

How to Interpret the Price Per Credit Hour:

The cost per credit hour offers useful information about how financially efficient various courses or academic programmes are. How to interpret the price per credit hour is as follows:

Cost-Effectiveness: A course or programme is more cost-effective if the price per credit hour is lower. It implies that you are getting the most out of your educational investment by paying less for each credit hour earned.

Comparison of Courses or Programmes: You can evaluate the financial effects of various courses or programmes by comparing their cost per credit hour. You can decide which courses are most cost-effective and fit into your spending plan and financial objectives.

Cost per credit hour: This information is useful while budgeting for your education. It enables you to calculate the overall cost of finishing a degree or programme based on the number of credits needed. You can use this data to establish budgetary plans and wise choices regarding your educational costs.

It's crucial to remember that while comparing educational

options, the price per credit hour is simply one factor to take into account. Additional elements including educational quality, institution repute, faculty specialization, job opportunities, and individual interests should also be considered. To make a well-rounded choice, consider the cost per credit hour together with these aspects.

Also bear in mind that prices per credit hour may change between universities, courses, and areas in India. It's crucial to have precise and current information from the particular educational institutions you're thinking about. By doing this, you can be confident that you have the most current and accurate information possible to decide wisely about your educational investments.

You can decide which courses or academic programmes are the most cost-effective by using the cost per credit hour method and taking the bigger picture into account. You get the ability to control your educational costs and make decisions that are consistent with your aims and financial goals.

CHAPTER Eighteen

Now, it's time to earn while you learn.

Finding Scholarships: Getting Money for Your Educational Journey

The Scholarship Search Formula, a step-by-step procedure to increase your chances of receiving scholarships in India, will be covered in this chapter. You can improve your chances of receiving financial aid and lessen the burden of college costs by setting aside a specific amount of hours each week to study and apply for scholarships. To assist you in successfully navigating the scholarship search process, we will offer real-world examples and in-depth advice.

Section 1: Planning Your Scholarship Search Strategy.

1.1 Determining Your Eligibility and Objectives

It's important to determine your goals and determine your eligibility before starting your scholarship quest. Take into account your extracurricular activities, personal qualities, and academic accomplishments that qualify you for scholarships. Determine the kind of scholarships that are appropriate for your course of study, professional aspirations, or other particular requirements by evaluating your educational objectives. You can focus on the scholarships that are most pertinent to you by being aware of your abilities and objectives.

Practical Illustration: Neha, an Indian high school student, wants to major in engineering. In order to find grants specifically for engineering students, she assesses her academic achievement, participation in STEM clubs, and leadership positions. She concentrates her search on grants that aid students pursuing engineering degrees and exhibit a dedication to volunteerism.

1.2 Choosing a Time Commitment That Is Realistic:

Success depends on setting aside a certain amount of time each week for scholarship research and applications. Make a timetable that allows for targeted scholarship search efforts after taking into account your current obligations, including those to your studies, extracurricular activities, and part-time work. Establish a reasonable time commitment that works with your schedule and guarantees steady advancement in your search.

Example in Practise: Raj, a college student, pledges to

devote 5 hours per week on scholarship application and study. He schedules time specifically for scholarship-related tasks on the weekends and makes use of his study breaks. Raj makes sure he constantly devotes time to his scholarship pursuit by adhering to his schedule.

Section 2: Researching Scholarships.

2.1 Investigate Government Scholarships:

To aid students in their academic endeavors, the Indian government provides a number of scholarships. The Ministry of Education, the Ministry of Social Justice and Empowerment, and different state governments offer research fellowships. To learn more about eligibility requirements, application procedures, and deadlines, visit government websites, scholarship portals, and academic institutions. Government scholarships frequently target particular groups, such as merit-based, minority communities, economically disadvantaged students, or particular academic disciplines.

Using the National Scholarship Portal (NSP) to research scholarships, postgraduate student Priya came across the Central Sector Scheme of Scholarships for College and University Students. To determine her eligibility, she looks over the application requirements and eligibility conditions. In order to find out if there are any additional chances available just for state residents, Priya also looks into the scholarships granted by her state's government.

2.2 Look into Private Scholarships:

Numerous private foundations, businesses, and charity organizations in India provide scholarships in addition to those provided by the government. To find appropriate opportunities, use trustworthy scholarship websites, scholarship directories, and online scholarship search engines. Specific qualifications for private scholarships may be determined by a candidate's academic standing, extracurricular activities, financial need, or other factors.

Example in Practice: Rohit, a student interested in a career in journalism, looks into the private scholarships provided by publications, journalistic associations, and media firms. He looks for scholarships that support his chosen field using online databases and scholarship search engines. Rohit also looks into internship and scholarship opportunities on the websites of well-known media organizations.

2.3 Local Scholarships:

Local communities frequently offer scholarships through nonprofits, corporations, and charitable people. To learn about local scholarship options, contact libraries, community centers, and educational organizations in your area. Your chances of winning may be higher because the candidate pool for these scholarships may be less.

Example: Manisha, a student from a small town, contacts the Rotary Clubs, community foundations, and local companies to ask for scholarships. She learns of a scholarship programme being offered by a nearby manufacturer in support of students pursuing technical education. Manisha emphasizes her love of technical knowledge and her dedication to the neighborhood when applying for the scholarship.

Section 3: Making Effective Scholarship Applications.

3.1 Create an outstanding resume or CV:

A strong curriculum vitae (CV) or resume is essential to highlight your accomplishments, abilities, and experiences. Your resume or CV should be tailored to highlight your academic success, extracurricular activities, leadership positions, volunteer work, and relevant employment experiences. Showcase your abilities and how they fit the criteria for the scholarship.

Example in Practice: Sanjay, a student in his first year of college, puts together a thorough resume that shows his academic successes, research endeavors, internship experiences, and leadership roles in student organizations. In order to demonstrate his dedication to social problems and community involvement, he also highlights his volunteer work for a nearby NGO.

3.2 Writing a strong personal statement or essay is a requirement for many scholarship applications:

since it allows the scholarship committee to assess your motivation, objectives, and potential influence. Create a strong essay that highlights your individual talents, experiences, and future objectives. Emphasize your enthusiasm, dedication, and how winning the scholarship would help you advance both academically and personally.

Example in Practise: Meena, a student of art, composes

a potent essay outlining her love of creativity, her artistic path, and how receiving a scholarship would allow her to further her education and give back to the art world.

3.3 Get Strong Recommendations:

Ask for informative recommendation letters from professors, mentors, or employers that can attest to your academic prowess, character, and potential. Give these people specific directions and plenty of time to write the recommendations.

Practical Example: Deepak, a college student, asks his instructors to write recommendations for him based on their knowledge of his academic standing and participation in research initiatives. He gives them a thorough rundown of the guidelines and application deadline for the scholarship.

Section 4: Application for Scholarships

4.1 Adhere to Directions Carefully:

The instructions for applying for scholarships should be carefully read and understood. Make sure to carefully fill out all the essential information and submit the application by the due date.

Anjali, a doctoral student, carefully examines the directions for the scholarship application, noting the needed paperwork, essay word counts, and submission method. Before submitting her application, she checks to make sure all of the fields are correctly filled in.

4.2 Track Application Deadlines:

Establish a mechanism for tracking application deadlines for scholarships. To guarantee that applications are submitted on time, set reminders and alerts.

Practical Example: Arjun, a student who is applying for several scholarships, keeps a spreadsheet with information about each scholarship, such as deadlines, specifications, and the status of submissions. In order to remember the application deadlines, he sets up calendar reminders.

4.3 Follow Up:

Monitor the scholarship application process and conduct additional research as necessary. Be ready for any possible interviews or requests for more paperwork.

Example in Practise: Meera, a candidate for a scholarship, checks her email frequently for developments regarding the scholarship she applied for. She swiftly replies to requests for interviews to set up the appointment and does the necessary preparations.

You can greatly improve your chances of receiving scholarships in India by using the Scholarship Search Formula and adhering to the offered real-world examples. Plan your search strategy for scholarships, do your due diligence, create compelling application materials, and submit your applications on time. The path to obtaining financial aid through scholarships calls for commitment, planning, and tenacity. You may successfully manage the scholarship search process and lessen the financial load of your education with constant work and a calculated approach.

CHAPTER

Nineteen

Allocating Part-Time Job Earnings: Juggling Income and Financial Obligations

In this chapter, we'll discuss the idea of putting some of the money you get from part-time work towards paying off student loans or other educational costs. In India, many students work part-time jobs to help pay for their education and other costs. Students can reconcile their short-term necessities with their long-term objectives by carefully allocating a portion of their earnings. We will explore the specifics of this allocation technique using real-world examples and in-depth advice.

Section 1: Understanding the Value of Part-Time Employment.

Working part-time can help students make money to pay for educational costs like tuition, books, study materials, and other costs associated with attending school. It promotes financial independence and lessens dependency on outside financing sources.

Rahul is a first-year engineering student in the real world. He works as a tutor part-time, assisting high school pupils with their coursework. Rahul makes a consistent income from his part-time employment by putting in a few hours a week, which he uses to pay for his school costs. He manages his academic expenses independently and lessens the financial strain on his family by using a portion of his income to pay for his textbooks, study materials, and lab equipment.

1.2 Getting Work Experience and Developing Skills:

Part-time jobs give students the chance to gain useful work experience while also honing crucial abilities like time management, communication, teamwork, and problem-solving. Their long-term professional prospects and employability can both benefit from these experiences.

Sneha is a college student who is majoring in business administration. She performs part-time customer service and inventory management duties at a nearby retail establishment. Sneha acquires real-world experience in customer service through her work, as well as knowledge of handling money and great communication abilities. These experiences not only help her financially but also benefit her future professional endeavors.

Section 2: Allocating Part-Time Job Earnings.

2.1 Evaluating Financial Needs and Goals:

It's critical to evaluate your financial needs and goals before allocating part-time employment earnings. Analyze your monthly costs, taking into account things like rent, utilities, travel, groceries, and other necessities. Establish the amount necessary to meet these costs as well as any other financial objectives, such as student loan repayment or the saving for future schooling.

Aarti is a graduate student who is seeking a master's in computer science. In order to comprehend her monthly spending, she develops a thorough budget. Rent, utilities, food, transportation, and a small sum for recreation are all included in Aarti. Aarti resolves to put 40% of the money she makes from her part-time work towards her university savings fund and the remaining 60% towards her monthly costs after calculating her outgoings. She is able to cover her urgent financial demands while prioritizing her long-term educational objectives thanks to this allocation approach.

2.2 Determining a Percentage Allocation:

Take into account assigning a certain portion of your earnings from a part-time employment to cover your educational costs or student loan payments. Depending on a person's situation and financial objectives, the proportion may change. A usual rule of thumb is to set aside roughly 50% of income for these uses, with the remaining 50% going towards living expenditures.

Practical Illustration: Karan is a finance major who works while attending school. He has a solid job as a data entry clerk and works part-time. Karan resolves to use 50% of the money he makes from his part-time work towards paying off his student loans. He arranges a monthly automated transfer of funds from his earnings to his loan account. His living costs, including rent, groceries, transportation, and personal expenses, will be covered by the remaining 50%. Karan is able to successfully manage his daily costs while making steady progress towards repaying his student debts thanks to this allocation technique.

2.3 Automating

The Allocation Process: Think about automating the allocation process to ensure consistency and prevent pressure to use the cash elsewhere. Set up automatic payments from your earnings from part-time work to specialized accounts or envelopes for paying loans or paying for college. This method streamlines the procedure and guarantees that the funds are utilized for their intended purpose.

Example in Practice: Deepika, a student and part-time employee, sets up automatic transfers from her bank account to two other accounts: one for her educational costs and the other for paying back student loans. Her monthly income is automatically deposited into these accounts in a set amount, doing away with the necessity for human transfers and lessening the possibility of money being misappropriated. Deepika is able to maintain discipline in her money management and successfully accomplish her financial goals because of her automated allocation technique.

Section 3: Taking Full Advantage of Benefits and Seeking Out New Opportunities

3.1 Monitoring and Analyzing Financial Development

Maintain a regular evaluation of your financial progress to make sure the money you've been given is being used effectively. Keep track of your spending, compare it to your budget, and make any required adjustments. You can find areas to minimize costs and increase your savings as a result of this practice.

Example in Practise: Sameer, a student managing his earnings from a part-time job, utilizes a smartphone app to monitor his expenses. He classifies his expenditure and compares it to his allotted budget, breaking it down into categories like grocery, travel, entertainment, and personal expenses. Sameer discovers places where he may decrease costs and increase his savings towards his financial objectives by keeping an eye on his spending. For instance, he realizes that choosing free or inexpensive activities will allow him to lower his entertainment costs without sacrificing enjoyment.

3.2 Seeking Additional Income options:

While setting aside a percentage of your earnings from part-time work is important, think about looking into additional income options to further increase your financial resources. Look for part-time jobs, internet gigs, or freelance work that fits your schedule and skill set.

Practical Example: During her leisure time, Priya, a student with a part-time job, works as a freelance writer. She can allocate a larger percentage of her new money from freelancing to school costs, which hastens her progress towards her financial objectives. Priya recognises her writing strengths and searches for writing tasks on websites that offer freelance opportunities and social media. In addition to meeting her financial necessities, the extra money helps her develop her talents and widen her network of contacts in the business world.

You can manage your finances well and work towards long-term financial objectives by setting aside a percentage of your part-time job earnings for paying off student loans or paying for educational expenses. The real-world examples presented in this chapter show how Indian students can reconcile their current necessities with their long-term goals. To maximize the benefits, keep track of your progress and look for more income options. Don't forget to evaluate your financial needs and goals, set a percentage allocation, automate the process, and monitor your progress. You may maximize your earnings from part-time jobs and attain financial stability while pursuing your studies with careful preparation and persistent effort.

CHAPTER

Twenty

Work experience and internships open up career opportunities

This chapter will go in-depth on the value of internships and part-time employment for students seeking to get real-world work experience. Internships provide a priceless chance to put academic understanding into practice, hone industry-specific skills, and investigate potential career routes. We will examine how internships and job experience can advance students' professional development and open doors to interesting career options through real-world examples and thorough explanations.

Section 1: Understanding the Value of Internships and Work Experience.

1.1 Bridging the Academic-Real World Gap:

Internships serve as a link between theoretical learning and practical implementation. They give students the chance to develop real-world skills, put theoretical ideas into practice, and comprehend how businesses function in a formal atmosphere. Students can see directly how their academic learning in terms of knowledge and abilities is applied in the workplace through job experience.

Example in Practice: Priya, a marketing student, lands a summer internship with a digital marketing firm. Priya gets exposed to numerous marketing tactics, social media initiatives, and client contacts during her internship. She gains knowledge of data analysis, marketing report creation, and campaign participation. The internship helps her better comprehend marketing concepts while also giving her useful skills that she can use in her future job.

1.2 Opportunities for Networking

Students have the opportunity to broaden their professional networks through internships and part-time work. They provide doors to future work chances and give access to professionals in the field, mentors, and colleagues. Internship networking can result in beneficial relationships and referrals for future job growth.

Example in Practise: Rahul, a student of computer science, is granted an internship with a prestigious IT firm. Rahul is actively interacting with his coworkers, going to networking events, and looking for guidance from seasoned professionals throughout his internship. Rahul develops a strong network of business contacts through these meetings, contacts who not only help him during his internship but also put him in touch with job openings after graduation.

Section 2: Benefits and Tips for Maximizing Internship and Work Experience.

Gaining Industry - Specific Skills: Students can get industry-specific skills that are highly desired in their chosen industries by participating in internships and part-time work. Working in a professional environment exposes students to tools, technologies, and best practices used in the business, which can greatly improve their employability.

Example in Practice: Smita, a renewable energy-focused engineering student, lands an internship at a solar energy business. Smita gains knowledge about project management, energy conversion technologies, and the installation of solar panels during her internship. She acquires practical expertise in building renewable energy systems and conducting energy audits. This hands-on experience improves Smita's prospects of landing a full-time job in the renewable energy sector and provides her with the information and abilities she needs to flourish in her area.

2.2 Examining Career Options and Defining Objectives:

Students get the chance to explore several career routes and clarify their future aspirations through internships and part-time employment. Students can determine their abilities, interests, and preferences by working in a variety of positions and industries, which will enable them to make well-informed judgments about their future career prospects.

Example in Practice: Ravi, a student of business administration, works part-time in a variety of fields, including marketing, human resources, and finance. Ravi decides to concentrate his career in finance after learning to love financial analysis through these encounters. Ravi can better comprehend the range of job alternatives thanks to exposure to diverse roles, which enables him to set his ambitions in line with them.

Section 3: Techniques for Finding Internships and Getting the Most Out of Work Experience

3.1 Researching and Applying for Internships:

In order to land worthwhile internships, students must proactively investigate businesses, sectors, and open internship positions. They should submit well-written applications that show their excitement and motivation, and they should customize their resumes and cover letters to highlight their relevant abilities and experiences.

Practical Illustration: Journalism student Neha wants to work in broadcast journalism. She investigates media companies, seeks out internship opportunities, and customizes her cover letter and resume to highlight her writing prowess and enthusiasm for narrative. Neha sends thoughtful applications to various news outlets and then follows up with tailored emails to show her interest. Her efforts are successful, and she is able to land an internship at a reputable news outlet where she may practice her skills in news reporting and production.

3.2 How to Get the Most Out of Your Internship Experiences:

Students should take a proactive stance in order to maximize the advantages of internships. They should actively participate in organizational learning opportunities, look for chances to take on difficult initiatives, and solicit feedback from colleagues and superiors. Developing close bonds with coworkers and mentors can also be a great source of advice and support.

Example in Practise: Arjun, a student of architecture, is granted an internship with a prestigious architectural firm. He eagerly seeks out opportunities to work on high-profile projects and accepts duties above and above those that are delegated to him. Arjun actively engages in design conversations and solicits input from more experienced architects. He gains notoriety inside the company for his aggressive approach and effort, and at graduation, he obtains a job offer.

By giving students actual experience, industry-specific skills, networking opportunities, and clarity on their future objectives, internships and work experience are essential in determining how students' careers will develop. Students in India can comprehend thc value of internships and discover techniques to gain relevant chances through the use of the real-world examples covered in this chapter. Students can develop a competitive advantage, improve their employability, and pave the road for a fruitful career path by actively participating in internships and part-time work.

CHAPTER Twentyone

Something Important you should know

Making Decisions Based on Opportunity Cost Understanding

We shall examine the idea of opportunity cost and its importance in decision-making in this chapter. By taking into account the advantages and drawbacks of various options, an understanding of opportunity cost aids people in making wise decisions. We will explore the idea of opportunity cost in the Indian context through real-world examples and thorough explanations, emphasizing its significance in both personal and professional decision-making.

Section 1: Understanding Opportunity Cost.

1.1 Definition of Opportunity Cost:

When one choice is chosen over another, opportunity cost refers to the value of the next best alternative that is lost. It stands for the possible advantages or chances that are given up in favor of the selected course of action. Individuals can examine trade-offs and reach judgements that are in line with their goals and priorities by being aware of the opportunity cost.

Ramesh, a college student, must choose between going to a concert with his friends and studying for a forthcoming exam during that time. The prospective benefit of using that time to prepare and get a better exam score than the opportunity cost of going to the concert. Ramesh considers the advantages and trade-offs and thinks that studying is preferable because it has a lower opportunity cost than going to the concert.

1.2 The Importance of Opportunity Cost:

Making wise judgements requires an understanding of opportunity cost. People can evaluate the long-term effects of their decisions by taking into account the benefits and trade-offs of various possibilities. It supports goal prioritization, resource optimisation, and utility maximization.

Example in Practise: Meera, a working professional, is thinking of enrolling in a part-time MBA programme while maintaining her position. She examines the money commitment, time commitment, and prospective professional progression to determine the opportunity cost of enrolling in the programme. Meera is aware that getting an MBA will take a lot of time and money, but that the opportunity cost of doing so could be limited professional advancement and lost networking chances. With this knowledge, Meera chooses to apply to the MBA programme after balancing the prospective advantages and missed opportunities.

Section 2: Opportunity Cost Influencing Factors

2.1 Time:

Opportunity cost is greatly influenced by time. You cannot use time spent on one activity for another. People can estimate the opportunity cost and make judgements that take into account the time needed for various possibilities.

Anjali, an entrepreneur, must choose whether to devote her efforts to growing her current business or investigating a new opportunity. She weighs the time needed to pursue each option against its potential for development and profitability. Anjali is aware of the potential growth and development of her current business as the opportunity cost of concentrating on a new enterprise. In light of this, she makes the choice to devote her time and resources to growing her present company.

2.2 Financial Considerations:

Money matters a lot when it comes to opportunity cost. People can assess the prospective returns and trade-offs of various solutions by analyzing the financial investment necessary.

Rajesh is thinking about making an investment in either

stocks or real estate. He evaluates both choices' potential returns, hazards, and financial requirements. Rajesh understands that the potential growth and rental income he could have made from real estate would have been the opportunity cost of investing in equities. Rajesh carefully considers his options before deciding to engage in real estate, taking into account the opportunity cost of forgoing stock investments as well as any prospective long-term gains.

Section 3: Evaluation of Opportunity Cost in Decision-Making.

3.1 Identifying Alternatives:

People must recognise and evaluate the potential alternatives in order to appropriately evaluate opportunity costs. People can analyze the potential advantages, hazards, and trade-offs of each solution by taking into account a variety of options.

Shalini wishes to get a new smartphone, for instance. She recognises many models and contrasts their traits.

Client feedback, costs, and prices. Shalini understands that the potential savings or investments she could have made with the price difference would be the opportunity cost of selecting a more expensive model. Shalini makes the decision to select a model based on her assessment, taking into account the opportunity cost of spending more on a more expensive choice.

3.2 Weighing Trade-Offs and Benefits:

People can make wise selections by evaluating the

advantages and trade-offs of each option. People can assess the opportunity cost and prioritize their decisions by taking into account the potential benefits and trade-offs associated with various alternatives.

Example in Practice: Sanjay has been given two job offers, one with a greater pay but longer hours and the other with a slightly lower pay but a better work-life balance. Sanjay compares the financial advantages of each option to the quality of life and the time spent with family in order to determine the opportunity cost of each choice. Sanjay decides to take the position with a better work-life balance after weighing his priorities and realizing the potential cost of forgoing some income in exchange for increased personal wellbeing.

Making wise judgements in both personal and professional life requires an understanding of and evaluation of opportunity cost. People can prioritize their objectives, make better use of their resources, and accomplish better results by taking into account the potential advantages, trade-offs, and opportunity costs associated with various possibilities. Individuals in India can improve their decision-making skills and make decisions that are consistent with their values and goals by using the applicable examples and thorough explanations included in this chapter.

CHAPTER

Twentytwo

Government schemes for Students to Earn and Learn

Pradhan Mantri Kaushal Vikas Yojana (PMKVY): With the help of the Pradhan Mantri Kaushal Vikas Yojana (PMKVY), 500 million young people are expected to receive training by the year 2022. The Ministry of Skill Development and Entrepreneurship is running the programme. This programme aims to develop young people in a variety of skill areas. Government-approved training centers deliver the instruction. Throughout the training time, the trainees get a stipend.

National Apprenticeship Promotion Scheme (NAPS): This Scheme was established in 1994 with the intention of encouraging young people to pursue apprenticeships. The Ministry of Labour and Employment is running the programme. This programme aims to encourage youth to pursue apprenticeships. Students may receive training through this programme in a variety of businesses and industries. During the training time, they receive a stipend.

Skilling India Mission: It was established in 2015 with the objective of developing a competent workforce in India. The Ministry of Skill Development and Entrepreneurship is carrying out the task. The goal of this mission is to develop a skilled labor force in India. The government is working to train millions of young people in many skill areas as part of this mission.

National Skill Development Corporation (NSDC): In order to encourage skill development in India, the National Skill Development Corporation (NSDC) was founded in 2009. Government and the commercial sector collaborate on NSDC as a public-private partnership. The Skilling India Mission must be carried out by this corporation. The NSDC helps establish new training institutes and provide financial support to existing training facilities.

Benefits & Limitations of Each Schemes

Pradhan Mantri Kaushal Vikas Yojana

Benefits:

Gives young people skills in fields that are in demand aids in youth employment increases youth employability gives young people a stage on which to display their talents

Limitations:

It's possible that not all training providers offer training of the same caliber.

The programme might not be able to assist every young person in need.

The programme might not be able to satisfy the need for qualified workers in the economy.

National Apprenticeship Promotion Scheme.

Benefits:

Gives young people on-the-job training and supports their employment increases adolescent employability and provides a stage for them to display their abilities

Limitations:

There might not be enough apprenticeships available to meet demand.

It's possible that not all firms provide apprenticeship

programmes of the same caliber.

The programme might not be able to assist every young person in need.

Skilling India Mission

Benefits:

aims to develop a qualified workforce in India gives young people a platform to learn new skills and increases their employability by helping them find jobs

Limitations:

The programme might not be able to assist every young person in need.

The programme might not be able to satisfy the need for qualified workers in the economy.

It's possible that not all training providers offer training of the same caliber.

National Skill Development Corporation (NSDC)

Benefits:

Encourages India's talent development gives young people a platform to learn new skills increases young employability and aids in their employment

Limitations:

Because NSDC is a public-private collaboration, the

government does not provide all of its funding.

This may make it challenging for NSDC to assist all young people who require support.

It's possible that not all training providers offer training of the same caliber.

The steps for applying for the above-mentioned schemes are as follows:

Pradhan Mantri Kaushal Vikas Yojana (PMKVY):

Visit the PMKVY website and search for the training program that you are interested in.

Click on the "Apply Now" button and fill out the application form.

Upload the required documents, such as your proof of identity, proof of age, and educational certificates.

Submit your application and wait for approval.

National Apprenticeship Promotion Scheme (NAPS):

Visit the NAPS website and search for the apprenticeship program that you are interested in.

Click on the "Apply Now" button and fill out the application form.

Upload the required documents, such as your proof of

identity, proof of age, and educational certificates.

Submit your application and wait for approval.

Skilling India Mission:

Visit the Skilling India Mission website and search for the training program that you are interested in.

Click on the "Apply Now" button and fill out the application form.

Upload the required documents, such as your proof of identity, proof of age, and educational certificates.

Submit your application and wait for approval.

National Skill Development Corporation (NSDC):

Visit the NSDC website and search for the training program that you are interested in.

Click on the "Apply Now" button and fill out the application form.

Upload the required documents, such as your proof of identity, proof of age, and educational certificates.

Submit your application and wait for approval.

Conclusion

Dr. Mukul Agrawal's book, Money & You: Building a Strong Relationship with Money, is a game-changing manual that teaches readers how to develop positive, empowered relationships with their money. Dr. Mukul Agrawal, who has 19 years of expertise in the finance sector, wrote this book to address the particular difficulties that individuals have in efficiently managing their money.

We have looked at a wide range of financial ideas, tactics, and real-world examples that can completely alter the way we manage our money over the chapters. This book provides us with the knowledge and tools required to make informed decisions and take control of our financial future, covering topics like budgeting, savings, debt management, and investing.

Money & You dives into a number of important aspects of personal finance and provides tips and strategies that can help us change our spending patterns and outlook on money. Dr. Mukul Agrawal places a strong emphasis on the need of comprehending our own personal values and connecting them to our financial objectives. We can develop a prosperity mindset that opens the door to financial success by adopting a positive perspective on wealth creation, engaging in acts of appreciation, and letting go of limiting attitudes about money.

Dr. Mukul Agrawal recognises the distinct financial difficulties that students encounter and offers specific chapters to address their requirements. Students can discover helpful advice to manage their finances while continuing their education, from looking into scholarship options and part-time jobs to acquiring real-world work experience through internships.

The book also outlines numerous government programmes and initiatives designed to aid in the financial support of students. The eligibility requirements, application procedures, and advantages of these programmes are clarified by Dr. Mukul Agrawal, enabling students to make the most of the resources at their disposal and lessen their financial load.

Dr. Mukul Agrawal makes sure the information in Money & You is pertinent to and understandable in the Indian context. Readers may relate to the content and apply the ideas to their own life with the use of real-world examples and case studies based on the Indian financial scene. By doing this, Dr. Mukul Agrawal fills the gap between theory and actual application, making it possible for readers to use the ideas to their advantage.

It is crucial to understand that the power is in our hands as we get to the end of Money & You. Dr. Mukul Agrawal has given us the information, resources, and direction we need, but it is up to us to put these tactics into practice in our daily lives. We can embark on a revolutionary financial journey where money becomes a tool for progress, stability, and eventually, a full life, by implementing the principles and practices taught in this book.

The book Money & You - Building a Strong Relationship with Money is a catalyst for both personal and financial transformation, to sum up. For anyone looking to improve their financial security, Dr. Mukul Agrawal's knowledge, along with his personable writing style and useful examples, makes this book a great resource. Let's take the advice given in these pages to heart and set out on the road to financial success, where money serves as a tool to live a life of meaning, freedom, and abundance.

Thank You

Dear Reader

As Money & You: Building a Strong Relationship with Money comes to a conclusion, I want to sincerely thank each and every one of you for joining me on this life-changing adventure. It has been my honor and delight to help you understand the complexities of personal finance and provide you the tools you need to develop a solid and successful relationship with money.

I want to start by expressing my gratitude for your confidence in me. I was inspired to put my knowledge and experience into the pages of this book by your consistent support and conviction in the value of financial education. Your dedication to enhancing your financial situation motivates me and serves as a reminder of the significance of the job we are doing jointly.

I'm very appreciative of the chance to share my 19 years of financial experience with you. My earnest wish is that the knowledge and skills you acquire through the insights, methods, and real-life examples presented in this book will enable you to successfully navigate the complicated world of personal finance. May you feel confident in your ability to make wise choices, establish worthwhile financial goals, and take charge of your financial destiny.

I want to express my gratitude to my team for all of their hard work in making sure that this book gets to you in the best possible condition. They have been essential in making Money & You a reality because of their commitment to excellence, expertise, and dedication. They have never wavered in their support, and I will always be grateful for that.

Also receiving my gratitude are my family and friends who have supported me during this trip. My enthusiasm for financial education has been stoked by your consistent support, encouragement, and understanding, and you have made it easier for me to stay committed to my objective. I appreciate you being my sources of courage and motivation.

Finally, I want to recognise the importance of information and the positive influence it may have on our lives. I urge you to never stop learning, to stay curious, and to keep seeking information. Remember that acquiring sound financial knowledge is a lifelong effort, and that you may successfully manage the constantly shifting financial world by remaining knowledgeable and flexible.

My sincere aim is that Money & You has given you the tools you need to make sound financial decisions as well as sparked a desire within you to take charge of your financial future. May this book act as a catalyst for good change, guiding you towards a life of plenty, safety, and contentment.

Thank you once more for being a part of this amazing adventure. Your dedication to improving your financial situation is an investment not just in yourself but also in a chain reaction that has the potential to benefit your loved ones and future generations.

I wish you a future full of success, financial abundance, and most importantly, a life lived on your terms.

Thank you so much,

Dr. Mukul Agrawal